CAVENDISH PRA(

GW01158713

Procedure in Courts and Tribunals

SECOND EDITION

JOHN BOWERS QC AND IAN GATT
LITTLETON CHAMBERS
TEMPLE
LONDON

SERIES EDITOR
CM BRAND, SOLICITOR AND LECTURER IN LAW,
UNIVERSITY OF LIVERPOOL

Cavendish
Publishing
Limited

London • Sydney

Second edition first published in Great Britain 2000 by Cavendish Publishing Limited, The Glass House, Wharton Street, London WC1X 9PX, United Kingdom

Telephone: +44 (0) 20 7278 8000   Facsimile: +44 (0) 20 7278 8080

E-mail: info@cavendishpublishing.com

Visit our Home Page on http://www.cavendishpublishing.com

First published by Longman Law, Tax and Finance

Bowers, John, 1956–
Procedure in courts and tribunals – 2nd ed – (Practice Notes series)
1 Administrative procedure – England   2 Administrative procedure – Wales
I Title II Gatt, Ian
347.4'2'05

ISBN 1 85941 307 2

Printed and bound in Great Britain

This book is dedicated to the memory of H Sherman 1900–97

Preface

The aim of this book is not to set out the whole of civil and criminal procedure but to isolate and summarise those areas of practice which a young practitioner is likely to meet at the outset of his or her career. It is intended as a first reference point and signpost. This book appears at a time of great changes in the civil justice system and we make references to these where appropriate. The authors wish to thank Elizabeth Smaller, Howard Daley, Jeremy Morgan, Jenny Gardiner, Susan Doris, Sally Cowan and Tanya Robinson who have contributed material for the book.

John Bowers QC and Ian Gatt
1 October 1999

Contents

1 Basic Information

It is impossible in a short book to cover the entire scope of all the different courts and tribunals. Instead, we examine these topics as particular matters to note in certain of the courts and the most important specialised tribunals: general jurisdiction, procedure, principal rules and central offices.

1.1 Civil courts

1.1.1 High Court

This is divided into three divisions in which matters are assigned by the Supreme Court Act 1981 (the 'SCA').

Chancery Division

This division deals with matters relating to the administration of estates of deceased persons, bankruptcy, copyright, replacement of executor, guardians, sale of land, mortgages, partnerships, patents, probate, rectification, registered designs, trade marks and trusts. Subdivisions of the Chancery Division include the Bankruptcy Registry, Companies Court and the Patents Court.

Queen's Bench Division

This is concerned exclusively with matters relating to Admiralty, habeas corpus and judicial review. It is subdivided into the Commercial Court and Technology and Construction Court Business. There is much overlap between the Chancery and Queen's Bench Divisions in matters not specifically assigned to one or the other, for example, contractual claims.

Family Division

Matters dealt with in the Family Division include wardship, guardianship, adoption, affiliation and legitimacy proceedings, matrimonial actions and non-contentious probate cases.

The High Court sittings are in four terms:

- Michaelmas (October to December);
- Hilary (January to March);
- Easter (second Tuesday after Easter to the Friday before the Spring Bank Holiday);
- Trinity (second Tuesday after the Spring Bank Holiday to the 31 July). Some vacation judges sit in August for urgent business.

Procedure in the High Court is governed by the SCA 1981 and the Civil Procedure Rules 1998 (the 'CPR').

The CPR came into force on 26 April 1999. Subject to the transitional provisions (CPR Pt 51; Practice Direction – Transitional Arrangements), they apply in both the High Court and County Court. They mark a significant change in the culture of litigation. The CPR, together with the Practice Directions which have been issued, are intended to be a self-contained procedural code, although some provisions of the former Rules of the Supreme Court 1965 (the 'RSC'), formerly contained in the Supreme Court Practice, and the County Court Rules 1981 (the 'CCR'), formerly contained in the County Court Practice, still prevail. CPR Pt 50 deals with the extent to which the RSC and the CCR still apply.

It is not possible in this book to detail all the changes made by the CPR. We shall, however, examine the principal changes which have been made. For further information on the CPR, reference should be made to *The Civil Procedure Rules,* 1999, Sweet & Maxwell, *The Civil Court Practice,* 1999, Butterworths and *Blackstone's Guide to the Civil Procedure Rules,* 1999, Blackstone.

The CPR apply to cases in the county court as well as the High Court. The allocation of cases between the High Court and the County Court is explained in Practice Direction (PD 7) – How to Start Proceedings. Cases can be commenced in either the High Court or the county court, but:

- proceedings (whether for damages or a specified sum) cannot be commenced in the High Court unless the value of the claim is

£15,000 or more. In personal injury claims, the value of the claim must be at least £50,000;

- if a specific enactment requires a claim to be commenced in either the county court (for example, a claim under the Consumer Credit Act 1974) or the High Court (for example, an application for judicial review), then it must be commenced in the appropriate court;

- subject to the above, a claim should be started in the High Court if the claimant believes that it ought to be dealt with by the High Court by reason of:

  - the amount in dispute; or

  - the complexity of the facts, legal issues, remedies or procedures involved.

For a useful flowchart detailing the course of a claim under the CPR, see Kuljit Bhogal, *Dealing with Cases Justly – The Civil Procedure Rules* (1999) 149 NLJ 642, pp 642–43.

1.2   Criminal courts

1.2.1 Crown Court

In the Crown Court, a judge sits with a jury to hear cases either triable on indictment or where a defendant has exercised his right to trial by jury. The Crown Court also acts as the appeal court against both sentences and convictions by magistrates. In appeals against conviction, the case is re-heard not by a jury but by a judge and two to four lay magistrates.

1.2.2 Magistrates' court

This is the lowest court in the criminal justice system and the one in which most criminal cases are tried. Summary cases are heard by a bench of three (usually lay) magistrates. If a case is more serious, it is committed to the Crown Court.

1.3   Rights of audience

The rights of audience in the courts may be the subject of wide ranging reform. The present structure is as follows.

High Court

Only barristers or solicitors with the requisite advocacy qualification may appear in open court, but solicitors may appear in formal and unopposed applications such as reading out a statement in open court in defamation proceedings (see *Practice Direction* [1986] 1 WLR 645), certain bankruptcy cases and on the hearing of judgment summonses in the Family Division. In chambers, any legal representative may appear.

County court

Both solicitors and barristers may appear in the county court. As in the High Court, any legal representative may appear in chambers.

Tribunals

Normally, any representative may appear. For example, at an Immigration Appeal Tribunal the litigant may appear in person or, alternatively, a solicitor, barrister or counsellor from the UK Immigration Advisory Service.

Tribunal	Jurisdictions	Panel Constitution	Important Notes	Main Rules
Criminal Injuries Compensation Authority	Compensation for victims of rape, assault, arson, explosions or those injured in the course of apprehending an offender or preventing the commission of an offence.	Consists of practising lawyers or former holders of judicial office; papers are initially passed to a single member but he may refer it to a three person board.	Awards are only payable if the application is made within three years of the incident save in 'exceptional cases'. Right of appeal to a Queen's Bench judge.	Criminal Justice Act 1988, ss 108–17.
Immigration Appeal Tribunal (IAT)	Hears conditions attached to entry or leave to remain in the UK, appeals against exclusion, deportation and directions for removal from the UK, also has jurisdiction if a decision was taken 'not in accordance with the law' or applicable immigration rule.	Consists of three persons, one of whom must be a solicitor or barrister.	Witnesses remain outside the hearing room; full opening speeches are rarely made and only official interpreters are permitted.	Immigration Appeals Act 1969; Immigration Rules and Immigration Appeals (Procedure) Rules 1984 (SI 1984/2041).

Employment Tribunals	Have jurisdiction over unfair dismissal, redundancy payments, sex and race discrimination and the Employment Rights Act 1996.	Consists of three members: a legally qualified chairperson, as well as a representative of both the employers and the employee.	Most claims go to an ACAS conciliation officer who attempts to achieve settlement. Settlement is only effective to prevent further claims if achieved in this way. Costs are only awarded if a party behaves frivolously, vexatiously or otherwise unreasonably. Legal aid is available only for an appeal to the Employment Appeal Tribunal.	Employment Tribunal (Constitution and Rules of Procedure) Regulations 1993 (SI 1993/2165).
Mental Health Review Tribunal	Have power to discharge or order delayed discharge, to recommend leave, transfer to another facility or into guardianship. Can make recommendations to the Home Secretary and can reclassify the mental disorder which the patient is suffering from.	Consists of a president, who is a legal member, as well as a medical practitioner and a lay member.	ABWOR is available. The Law Society maintains a panel of legally qualified people approved by them. Hearings are held in private unless the patient requests a public hearing and the tribunal agrees.	Mental Health Act 1983; Mental Health Review Tribunal Rules 1983 (SI 1983/942).

Rent Assessment Committees (RAC)	RAC hear appeals from rent officers and determine disputes relating to purchase notices served by tenants on leaseholders wishing to exercise the 'right of first refusal' under the Landlord and Tenant Act 1987, Pt I.	Consists of a lawyer, a valuer and one lay person.	The tribunal normally inspects the premises in question on the day of the hearing.
Rent Tribunal (RT)	RT registers rents in respect of restricted contracts and delays in the operation of notices to quit served on restricted contract occupants whose tenancies/licences commenced before 28 November 1980.		
Leasehold Valuation Tribunal (LVT)	LVT decides price and rent payable by long lessee on enfranchisement or amount of compensation due to long lessee on a loss of rights due to landlord's redevelopment.		

Rent Assessment Committees (England and Wales) (Rent Tribunal) Regulations 1980 (SI 1980/1700); the Rent Act 1977, Landlord and Tenant Act 1987 and the Housing Act 1980.

Social Security Appeal Tribunals	Disputes arising out of claims to job seekers' allowance and social security benefits, statutory sick pay, maternity pay, etc.	Consists of one part time, legally qualified chairperson and two lay members.	A notice of appeal must be lodged within three months of the Adjudicating Officer's (AO) decision. The claimant will receive from the DSS a form with the terms of the decision, grounds of appeal, a statement of the relevant facts by the AO along with any submissions listing statutory provisions and relevant decisions of commissioners. Hearings are held in public unless the chairman is satisfied that intimate facts may have to be disclosed. The Tribunal has investigatory functions and evidence is not given on oath.	Social Security (Adjudication) Regulations 1986 (SI 1986/2218); Social Security Commissioners Procedure Regulations 1987 (SI 1987/214).

2 Time Limits

2.1 General considerations

Failures on the part of practitioners to comply with time limits probably cause more adverse judicial comment and give rise to more professional negligence claims than any other professional errors. For these reasons alone, a knowledge of, and compliance with, the main time limits is essential for any practitioner.

The two main areas of importance are the time limits imposed by the substantive law relating to limitation and those laid down in the CPR.

2.2 Limitation periods

2.2.1 Practice and procedure

In any particular case, unless you are sure of the appropriate limitation period, you should research the law appropriate to limitation at the first possible opportunity. (For a comprehensive consideration of this area of the law, see Josling, JF, *Limitation Periods*, 1994, London: Sweet & Maxwell). There are many areas of law where the time within which proceedings must be commenced is surprisingly short. For example, s 111(2) of the Employment Rights Act 1996 stipulates that a complaint of unfair dismissal must be made to an Employment Tribunal within three months from the effective date of termination, subject to an extension of time if it was not reasonably practicable to present the complaint within this period. Similarly, if proceedings have been commenced against your client, check that they are not statute barred. If the question of limitation is to be taken against the claimant, it should be raised at the earliest possible opportunity. In some cases (for example, the law relating to unfair dismissal), late institution of proceedings will deprive the tribunal of its jurisdiction so that, even if the respondent did not take the point, the Employment Tribunal would be unable to adjudicate upon the claim. In High Court proceedings, however, a party who wishes to resist a claim on the grounds of expiration of the relevant period of limitation must formally do so by raising it in his pleading: CPR 17.1 (formerly RSC Ord 18, r 8(1)).

Limitation periods are not only significant in the context of commencing and defending proceedings. They also become relevant in the context of the conduct of proceedings when an application is made to dismiss an action for delay.

2.2.2 Sanctions

The court has power pursuant to the CPR to strike out an action or statement of case (formerly a pleading) for default in a number of instances; for example, CPR 3.4(2)(c) (strike out of pleading for failure to comply with a rule, practice direction or court order).

The CPR contains a wide range of sanctions to deal with non-compliance with its provisions and delay. These vary from striking out the claim or defence to imposing a sanction which prevents the defaulting party from, for example, relying upon evidence served late or in a defective form. It is likely that the courts will readily apply their new sanctions. Pre-CPR cases, for example, *Arbuthnot Latham Bank Ltd v Trafalgar Holdings Ltd* [1998] 2 All ER 11 indicated the courts' willingness to take into account the effect of a defaulting party's delays on other court users as well as the other parties to the litigation. This approach is recognised in the overriding objective (CPR 1.1), that is, recognising the importance of taking into account when dealing with cases 'the need to allocate resources to other cases'.

Given the radical approach of the CPR to litigation, it is likely that the approach adopted in pre-CPR cases to striking out for want of prosecution will be re-evaluated and a more draconian stance adopted.

2.2.3 Is the claim time barred?

One of the first matters which the solicitor will have to establish from his client when taking original instructions is whether the claim is time barred. In order to answer this question, the following information must be obtained.

(1) What is the client's cause of action?

The answer to this can only be elicited from the client by thorough questioning and by considering all the relevant documentation. Once this has been done, the material facts of the case will be apparent and from them the potential causes of action should be evident.

(2) When did the cause of action accrue?

This is probably the most difficult of the five questions. The straightforward answer is that the cause of action generally accrues at the earliest moment at which an action could have been instigated. In these circumstances, there must be a potential claimant, a potential defendant and all the essential elements of the cause of action must be satisfied. In the ordinary run of breach of contract cases, the cause of action will accrue when the contract is breached, even though damage has not yet been sustained.

In respect of claims in tort, a distinction must be drawn between torts which are actionable *per se* without proof of damage (for example, trespass) and torts where actual damage to the claimant is an integral part of the cause of action (for example, negligence). In the former case, the cause of action will usually accrue at the time of the wrongful act; in the latter case, the cause of action will not be complete, and therefore actionable, until damage has been sustained.

Difficult questions may arise where damage has occurred but remained dormant, unknown to the potential claimant. In such cases, the latent damage provisions contained in s 14A of the Limitation Act 1980 may apply (see below).

(3) What is the appropriate period of limitation?

The following table sets out the principal causes of action and their respective limitation periods.

Cause of Action or Proceeding	Limitation Period
Carriage of goods by road	Action arising out of carriage of goods by road: one year. In the case of wilful misconduct: three years. See the Carriage of Goods by Road Act 1965.
Carriage by railway	In the case of a passenger involved in an accident: three years from the day after the accident. In the case of other claimants: three years from the day after the death of the passenger; or five years from the day after the accident, whichever is the earlier. In the case of consignment of goods: one year or three years. See the International Transport Conventions Act 1983.
Carriage by air	Written complaint must be made within seven days of damage or delay to cargo or baggage (except in the case of fraud on the part of the carrier). In the case of actions in respect of death or injury to passengers, destruction of or loss or damage to checked baggage or cargo, or delay: two years from the date of arrival at the destination or from the date on which the aircraft ought to have arrived or when the carriage ceased. See, also, the Carriage by Air Act 1961 and the Carriage by Air (Supplementary Provisions) Act 1962.
Contract	In the case of a simple contract (for example, not under seal or relating to land) excluding actions for equitable relief or relating to personal injuries: six years from the date on which the cause of action accrued. See, also, s 5 of the Limitation Act 1980.
Conversion	Six years from the date of the original wrongful act. See ss 3 and 4 of the Limitation Act 1980 for provisions relating to theft and successive conversions.
Deceit	Six years from the date the claimant discovered the deceit (or could with reasonable diligence have discovered it). See ss 2 and 32 of the Limitation Act 1980.
Defamation	One year from the date of publication (or re-publication) of the defamatory statement. Where the claimant did not begin proceedings within the appropriate period because all or any of the relevant facts were not known to him: one year (with the leave of the High Court from the earliest date when the claimant knew all the material facts).
Dependency under the Inheritance (Provision for Family and Dependents) Act 1975	Applications cannot be made without the leave of the court after the end of the period of six months from the date on which representation with respect to the estate is first taken out. See s 4 of the 1975 Act.

Employment: unfair dismissal	Within three months from the effective date of termination. (Dismissal in respect of unfair selection of strikers for re-engagement after industrial action: six months from the date of dismissal.) See, also, s 111(2)–(4) of the ERA 1996.
Race discrimination	Within three months from the date of the act complained of. See s 6(8)(1), (6) of the Race Relations Act 1976.
Sex discrimination	In most cases, three months from the date of the act complained of. See s 76(2) of the Sex Discrimination Act 1975.
Fatal accidents	Actions under the Fatal Accidents Act 1976 are not to be brought after three years from (a) the date of the death in respect of which the action is brought or (b) the 'date of knowledge' of the person for whose benefit the action is brought, whichever is the later. See s 12 of the Limitation Act 1980.
Judicial review	Applications for judicial review under RSC Ord 53 must be made promptly and in any event not more than three months from the date when the grounds for the application first arose. See RSC Ord 53, r 4 (CPR Sched 1).
Nuisance	Three years in the case of an action in respect of personal injuries. In other cases, six years.
Personal injuries	Where an action is maintained in negligence, nuisance or breach of duty and the damages claimed consist of or include damages in respect of personal injuries to any person no action is to be brought after three years from (a) the date on which the cause of action accrued or (b) the 'date of knowledge' of the injured person, whichever is the later. 'Date of knowledge' is defined by s 14 of the 1980 Act. See, also, s 11 of the Limitation Act 1980.
Specialty	An action upon a specialty (that is, a bond, a contract under seal or a covenant) cannot be brought after 12 years from the date of the breach of the obligation. See s 8(1) of the Limitation Act 1980.
Tort	With the exception of actions in respect of personal injuries or defamation and claims for equitable relief, no action can be brought after six years from the date when the cause of action accrued. See s 2 of the Limitation Act 1980.

The latent damage provisions of s 14A of the Limitation Act 1980 extend the limitation period in respect of claims in non-personal injury negligence actions. In such cases, where the claimant had not or could not reasonably have discovered that damage had occurred, the normal limitation period of six years is extended to a period three years from the date on which the claimant knew or ought reasonably to have known of the facts about the damage. This period is, however, subject to a 'long stop' of 15 years from the date of the defendant's breach of duty.

Where a number of possible limitation periods apply, the question of which prevails will have to be determined by looking at the respective provisions of the relevant statutes.

In many matters (particularly those in the field of administrative law involving the exercise of decision making powers under delegated legislation and appeals from such decisions), the time limits imposed upon individuals may be surprisingly short – usually three months – and care should be taken to research the legislation in each particular case.

(4) Has the appropriate period of limitation expired?

This question simply involves the mathematical exercise of calculating whether the appropriate period of time has elapsed since the date when the cause of action accrued. If proceedings have already been commenced, the question will arise: were they commenced within the limitation period? It is the date when proceedings are started and not the date of their service which is the effective date for these purposes. Proceedings are started when the court issues a claim form at the request of a claimant: CPR 7.1. Where the claim form as issued is received in the court office on a date earlier than the date on which it is issued by the court, the claim is 'brought' for the purposes of the Limitation Act 1980 and any other statute on that earlier date: PD 7, para 4.1. If time would otherwise expire on a date upon which the court is closed, proceedings commenced upon the day when the court is next open will be commenced on time: *Pritam Kaur v S Russel & Sons Ltd* [1973] QB 336.

(5) Is this an appropriate case for extending the period of limitation?

If the limitation period has ostensibly expired, it will be necessary to consider whether the claimant can rely upon any provisions extending or suspending the running of time. The principal provisions dealing with the enlargement of time are:

Disability

The 1980 Act deems a person to be under a 'disability' if they are an infant (that is, under 18 years old) or of unsound mind (s 38 of the Limitation Act 1980). The general rule established by s 28 of the 1980 Act is that if at the time any right of action accrued (for which a period of limitation is prescribed by the 1980 Act) the person to whom it accrued was under a disability, the limitation period is extended to six years from the date when he ceased to be under a disability or died. The exceptions to the general rule are personal injuries or death whereby the relevant extension is only three years, not six (s 28(6) of the 1980 Act) and latent damage cases covered by s 14A of the 1980 Act whereby the limitation period is three years from the date the claimant ceased to be under a disability.

Personal injuries or death

Section 33 of the 1980 Act gives the court a wide discretion to disapply the normal period of limitation set out in s 11 of the 1980 Act if it appears equitable to do so having regard to the balance of prejudice to the claimant and the defendant. This, in practice, is one of the most important provisions extending time. The material factors in the exercise of the court's discretion are:

(1) The length of, and the reasons for, the delay on the claimant's part.

(2) Having regard to the delay, the extent to which the evidence likely to be adduced is likely to be less cogent than if the case had been brought within the appropriate period. The court will take into account, for example, whether the defendant will be prejudiced by the effect of the passage of time upon the traceability of witnesses or the reliability of their evidence.

(3) The conduct of the defendant after the cause of action arose. Did the defendant refuse to assist the claimant in his requests for information to ascertain the nature of the defendant or facts material to his cause of action?

(4) The duration of any disability affecting the claimant which arose after the cause of action accrued.

(5) The extent to which the claimant acted promptly and reasonably once he knew he might have a claim for damages.

(6) The steps, if any, which the claimant took to obtain medical, legal or other expert advice and the nature of any such advice which he received. The court will look favourably on a claimant who sought

advice but was incorrectly advised and in reliance upon wrong advice allowed the limitation period to expire.

The discretion which the court has under s 33 is unfettered (see *Thompson v Brown* [1981] 1 WLR 744) but cannot extend time where proceedings were started and struck out and the new action is commenced out of the limitation period. No single factor is conclusive and the court should consider all relevant matters in determining which party has been most prejudiced. The fact that the claimant has received poor legal advice is a relevant, although not an overriding, consideration. Other relevant factors include:

- the fact that the defendant is insured in respect of the particular claim: *Firman v Ellis* [1978] 1 QB 886;
- the potential size of the claimant's claim;
- the claimant's prospects of success.

Fraud, deliberate concealment or mistake

Where the claimant's claim is either based on the fraud of the defendant or a fact material to it has been concealed by the defendant or the claim seeks relief from the consequences of a mistake, the period of limitation does not commence until the time when the claimant discovered (or ought reasonably to have discovered) the fraud, concealment or mistake (s 32 of the 1980 Act). This extension only applies to causes of action for which a limitation period is prescribed by the 1980 Act and does not apply to claims under the Fatal Accidents Act 1976.

2.2.4 Further considerations

In most cases, if the facts are fully ascertained at an early stage, proceedings can be commenced well within the limitation period. This will not always be possible and further investigation may have to be undertaken, especially in personal injury cases where, for example, the claimant's prognosis is uncertain or it is necessary to have pre-action discovery of medical records.

In any case where proceedings cannot be commenced immediately, it is good practice (if the limitation period has not yet expired) to make a prominent note somewhere on the solicitor's file or diary and in counsel's brief as to the date upon which the claim will become time barred. As that date approaches, a claim form should be issued to protect the client's position (it does not necessarily have to be served for four months after issue): CPR 7.5(2). It is good practice to maintain a master diary in the firm in case the relevant staff dealing with the matter are ill or on leave. After the claim form has been issued, care should be taken to ensure that its validity does not expire without it being renewed. It is only valid for a period of four months from its date of issue, unless extended under CPR 7.6.

If the limitation period will soon expire and papers are sent to counsel to settle proceedings, it is also good practice on the part of the solicitor to mark this fact prominently on the face of the brief and in the instructions. This avoids the risk of counsel failing to appreciate the urgency of the situation.

Equally, from the barrister's perspective, every set of papers should always be perused when they first arrive in chambers to ascertain whether an urgent response is needed. There are few experiences more frightening than opening a brief and realising that the limitation period has expired whilst papers have remained unopened on your desk.

You may consider the possibility of issuing and serving a claim form on the basis that the matter will not be proceeded with for the time being by agreement. It may be that the claimant is not required to serve particulars of claim unless and until the defendant gives (say) 28 days notice of the requirement for its service. This has advantages with regard to the accrual of interest on general damages for pain and suffering and loss of amenities.

If the limitation period has, on the face of it, expired, it will not be clear in some cases whether the claimant is entitled to an extension of time. For example, an issue may arise in a personal injury case as to when the injured person first had the knowledge of his injury required by s 14 of the Limitation Act 1980. In such cases, a claim form should be issued as soon as possible. This question can always be considered as a preliminary point if necessary.

2.3   Procedural time limits

The CPR prescribe many important time limits regulating the procedural aspects of conduct in both the High Court and the county court. There are also a number of important rules embodying principles which underlie the application of the procedural time limits.

It is very important to ensure that time limits for service of statements of case (formerly called pleadings), disclosure and other orders are complied with. In recent years the courts have adopted a much stricter approach to failures to comply with procedural time limits and requests for extensions of time. See, for example, *Beachley Property Ltd v Edgar*

[1997] PNLR 197; *The Mortgage Corpn Ltd v Sandoes* (1996) *The Times*, 27 December.

2.3.1 Computing time

In the High Court and the county court, time is computed in accordance with the provisions of CPR 2.8 to 2.10. These provisions set out the following rules:

(1) *Applicability.* CPR 2.8 shows how to calculate any period of time for doing any act which is required by the CPR, a Practice Direction or a judgment or order of the court.

(2) *Clear days.* A period of time expressed as a number of days is to be calculated as clear days. 'Clear days' means that, in computing the number of days the day on which the period begins, and if the end of the period is defined by reference to an event, the day on which that event occurs are not included. For example, notice of an application must be served at least three days before the hearing. If the application is to be heard on Friday 21 April, the last date for service of the notice is Monday 17 April.

(3) *Periods of five days or less.* Where the specified period is five days or less and that period includes a Saturday or Sunday or a Bank Holiday, Christmas Day or Good Friday, that day does not count.

(4) *Month.* 'Month' means calendar month (and not lunar month).

(5) *Time expiring on a day when the court office is closed.* When the period specified by the CPR, a practice direction or a judgment or order for doing any act expires on a day when the court office is closed, that act shall be done in time if it is done on the next day on which the court office is open.

It is important to note that CPR 2.9 also provides that, when a court gives a judgment, order or direction which imposes a time limit, the last date for compliance must, wherever practicable be expressed as a calendar date (rather than within a specified period of time) and include the time of day by which the act must be done. For example, an order should provide for the service of a list of documents 'by 4.30 pm on 9 July 1999' rather than 'within 14 days of the date of this order'.

2.3.2 Extending or abridging time

(1) Jurisdiction. In both the High Court and the county court, the court has a discretion to extend or abridge time for the doing of any act on

such terms as it thinks just (CPR 3.1(2)). An application may be made for an extension of time notwithstanding the fact that time for the doing of the act has already elapsed.

CPR 2.11 also provides that, unless the rules or a practice direction provides otherwise, the time specified by a rule or by the court for doing any act may be varied by written agreement of the parties.

Whilst the object of the court's power under CPR 3.1(2) is to enable the court to do justice between the parties and to avoid hardship as a result of non-compliance with time limits, in appropriate cases, if there is substantial and unexplained delay, the court may well refuse to exercise its discretion in favour of the defaulting party. Orders abridging time are rare and will not be granted if they would result in injustice to the other party.

(2) Procedure: CPR 23. In the High Court, an application to extend or abridge time should be made to the tribunal having jurisdiction of the matter. In most cases in London, this will be the master. The application will be heard by a district judge outside London. The application is made by application notice (or time application).

In term time, applications for extensions of time are made before a deputy master at 10.00 am. In vacation periods, however, applications are heard before the practice master at 10.30 am. In both cases, the applications are returnable three days from the date of issue (excluding Saturdays, Sundays and intervening holidays) unless the case is one of great urgency: see *Practice Direction (QBD) (Time Summonses)* [1989] 2 All ER 480.

If you intend to issue a time application, make sure that it is not listed at some later date as if it were an ordinary application. When you attend upon the hearing of the application, you may, depending upon the extent of the delay and the length of the extension of time required, be expected to explain the need for the extension of time and the reasons for any delay which has occurred. Be prepared to deal with these questions and, in a complicated or lengthy case, it may be appropriate to compile a chronology for the master setting out the relevant dates. If you do not have time to issue a time application before the expiry of the relevant period you should make it clear to the other side that if any action is taken prior to the application being determined by the master/district registrar, this will be brought to their attention at any subsequent hearing.

2.3.3 Important procedural time limits

The following table sets out the most important procedural time limits imposed by the RSC and CCR.

Nature of application or act required	Time limit and relevant authority/provision of RSC and CCR
Claimant serves particulars of claim	With the claim form or within 14 days after service of the claim form: CPR 7.4.
Defendant serves acknowledgment of service	Within 14 days of service of the particulars of claim: CPR 9.2(c) and Pt 10.
Defendant serves its defence	Within 14 days of service of the particulars of claim: CPR 9.2(b) and Pt 15.
Claimant serves its reply	With its allocation questionnaire: CPR 15.8 and 26.3.
Default judgment	If the defendant has not filed an acknowledgment of service or defence within 14 days of service of the particulars of claim: CPR 12.3.
Summary judgment	The claimant cannot apply for summary judgment unless the defendant has acknowledged service or filed a defence unless the court gives permission or a practice direction provides otherwise: CPR 24.4(1).
Service of application notice and applicant's evidence	The respondent to the application must be given 14 days' notice of the application and evidence relied upon: CPR 24.4(3).
Service of respondent's evidence	The respondent's evidence must be filed and served at least seven days prior to the hearing: CPR 24.5(3)(a).
Service of evidence in reply	Evidence in reply must be served not less than three days prior to the hearing: CPR 24.5(3)(b).
Appeal from master	Notice of appeal must be issued within 5 days after the judgment, order or decision appealed against was given or made and served within five days after issue: CPR Sched 1; RSC Ord 58, r 1(3).
Appeal from district judge	Notice of appeal must be issued within seven days after the judgment, order or decision appealed against was given or made and served within five days after issue: CPR Sched 1; RSC Ord 58, r 3(1).

Appeal to the Court of Appeal	Notice of appeal to be served within four weeks of the date upon which the judgment or order of the court below was sealed or otherwise perfected: CPR Sched 1; RSC Ord 59, r 4(1).
Setting down appeal – Court of Appeal	Within seven days after the later of service of the notice of appeal or the date on which the order of the court below was sealed or otherwise perfected: CPR Sched 1; RSC Ord 59, r 5(1).
Respondent's notice – Court of Appeal	To be served within 21 days of service of the notice of appeal: CPR Sched 1; RSC Ord 59, r 6(3).
Application for an Order	Application notice and evidence in support should be served at least three days before the court is to deal with the application, unless otherwise provided: CPR 23.7.
Part 36 Offer or Payment (formerly payment into court)	At any time after proceedings have been started (CPR 36.2(4)(a)), an offer made prior to commencement of proceedings may be taken into account if the provisions of CPR 36.10 are complied with: CPR 36.10.

3 Advising the Client

3.1 General points

Practitioners should never lose sight of the fact that the provision of advice to their clients will probably form the most substantial part of a practice. The style, form and content of the advice given will largely depend upon its intended recipients. The following points are, however, of general relevance.

(1) As a solicitor, always consider whether your client is eligible for legal aid or assistance under the green form scheme. If there is any real chance of the client being eligible for legal aid, he must be advised of the scheme, whether or not the solicitor who is advising undertakes legal aid work (*Guide to the Professional Conduct of Solicitors*, 1996, The Law Society, p 128).

(2) Ensure at the outset that your client appreciates the significance and consequences of potential proceedings both in financial and personal terms. This may include explaining:

   (a) whether costs will be recoverable if he is successful and, if they are, the difference between the 'standard' and 'solicitor and own client' bases of costs;

   (b) what the costs position will be if he loses and the position if the other side is legally aided (see Chapter 11);

   (c) the various stages of the action and how long it may take to get to trial.

(3) If the client is a new client, solicitors will usually wish to ask for money on account of costs to cover initial advice. This also has the advantage of focussing the client's mind on the legal implications of litigation at an early stage.

(4) When giving advice, remember your audience. Consider who is going to be the 'consumer' of your advice and draft it accordingly.

If it is to be directed to a lay person, do not use technical legal jargon or Latin tags. Write in plain, interesting and understandable English. If you use plain language, there is less risk of your client misinterpreting or not understanding what you said.

(5) Always check and re-check the substance of your advice to ensure that you have identified all the issues and advised upon them correctly. If you are unable to give a definitive answer, say so. Do not fudge the issues. If further information is required, spell out precisely what you need and, if necessary, why you need it. It may be appropriate to put this in the form of a question and answer checklist. For certain types of case, for example, personal injuries or employment cases, you can draw up certain standard questionnaires to elicit the material facts.

(6) If you advise orally, either in a meeting or over the telephone, always make a written record of the substance of the advice which you gave as soon as possible afterwards, if you did not advise from notes which you had already made.

(7) A practitioner should only advise a legally aided client to commence proceedings if he would advise a client paying his own costs to sue: *Kelly v London Transport Executive* [1982] 2 All ER 842.

Explain fully and clearly to the client:

• the full implications of the statutory charge on legal aid;

• the responsibility of the client to pay the solicitor and their own client bill independently of costs recovered from the other side; and the tactical uses and significance of payments in and Part 36 offers.

3.2   Establishing the facts

Before you advise your client, whether orally or in writing, first ascertain exactly what the facts of the matter are. Until you establish what the facts are (or what the disputes as to fact appear to be), you will not be able to define the issues for your consideration.

Gather together all the relevant documentation from your client. Don't necessarily be satisfied with the documents he gives you. Think what else there might be and probe to see if it exists. Try to establish from your client what the facts of the matter are. Again, consider whether he is giving you the full picture or simply providing you with the information which assists his case.

Make a list of the salient facts in short, numbered paragraphs. This will serve as a useful *aide-memoire* in the future. It will also highlight the areas where you do not have all the facts and enable you to make further enquiries. It is also useful, at the outset, to compile a chronology of the relevant dates. Do there appear to be any gaps? Establish what occurred in them. Include in the chronology any important items of correspondence and include a note of what the parties allegedly said to each other but which was not documented. A list of characters may also be helpful for future reference. Consider compiling a 'core bundle' of the key documents for use as the case develops.

3.3   Establishing the issues

Once you have mastered the material facts of the case, you need to work out what the issues are upon which your opinion is sought. Solicitors will have to establish what the client wants to achieve. What is his complaint or grievance? What remedy is he seeking? Counsel will generally be instructed as to the specific points upon which their advice is sought. Do not stray beyond the parameters of your initial instructions without express instructions from your solicitor. Do not, however, feel constrained by them, if there are obvious gaps. When you have established in general terms what is wanted, identify the specific legal and factual issues in a logical and coherent manner. Write down a framework within which the issues can be considered. This will form the structure of your advice. As a solicitor, you may wish to instruct counsel to give full advice, so that your initial advice may be quite general.

3.4   Advice

3.4.1 Written advice

Your overall objective must be to provide clear and concise advice to your client, as far as possible, in terms which he will understand. Although there is no right or wrong way of advising in writing, the following points can be used as a basis upon which to build your own personal style.

(1) Whether you are advising by letter or in a formal written opinion, keep your sentences short and concise and your prose (as far as the subject matter permits) interesting. Deal with separate matters in separate paragraphs. Avoid long paragraphs or convoluted conjunctions. Make your advice readable to both lawyers and laypeople.

(2) Set out what you have been asked to advise upon by the client. This not only gets the extent of your obligations clear in your own mind, but it also enables the client (and anyone else who may be shown the advice) to see that you are dealing with the points that he has raised. Counsel should always check through their instructions to establish that they have answered all the points upon which they were instructed to advise. Always consider whether there are other important matters upon which your advice should be given.

(3) Some practitioners find it helpful to state their conclusions in the first or second paragraph of their advice rather than keep their client 'in suspense'.

(4) In a first advice to a client, set out the salient facts which you have identified. If you have misunderstood anything this will give your client the opportunity of correcting your misapprehension before your advice is acted upon.

(5) Set out the specific issues which arise out of the facts you have established and the questions you have been asked to answer.

(6) Deal with the issues identified in a logical and coherent manner.

(7) State your conclusions in clear terms. If you cannot give a clear answer, explain why not. If the answer given is not based upon clear cut principles but depends upon the exercise of your judgment and your opinion, say so.

(8) If necessary, set out what further steps need to be taken in the matter. This can be done in the form of a chart or checklist.

3.4.2 Oral advice

Many of the points already mentioned apply with equal force whether you are advising in writing or orally. In the case of 'face to face' advice, it is also important to ensure that you are properly prepared. Make sure you have mastered the factual details and that you have carried out the necessary research to answer the points raised. An adviser who knows exactly what the case is about down to the finer point of detail inspires confidence in his client. Do not be pushed into advising too quickly if you have not mastered the basic facts.

If your client is unfamiliar with the process of litigation and the law, try and put him at his ease. Show sympathy for his problem. Give him the confidence that you will handle his case to the best of your abilities. Explain what has happened, what is going to happen and how long it may take! It is very important to give your advice (so far as is possible) in terms that your client can understand. Give him the opportunity to ask questions to clarify points that he doesn't understand. Explain to him what he can expect to achieve in the case.

Equally, if necessary, make it clear that legal proceedings are not a means of pursuing personal vendettas.

In complicated matters, make out a checklist of the matters you have to deal with in the course of giving your advice and tick them off as you dispose of them.

4 Statements of Case

4.1 General considerations

If you have little or no experience of drafting statements of case (formerly called 'pleadings'), it may be daunting to sit down with an empty piece of paper in front of you. One of the best ways to familiarise yourself with the form and style of the language of statement of case is simply to read other people's.

You should compile your own store of precedents which suit your style. Many practitioners photocopy statements of case which they have either drafted themselves or which they come across in practice and keep in an indexed file. A good store of precedents can substantially reduce the amount of time spent constructing the framework of the document. This advice applies not only to statements of case: it is also good practice to keep copies of well drafted trading terms and conditions, exclusion clauses, retention of title clauses, contracts of employment, sale agreements and so on for future reference.

In addition to the practitioner's own personal files, *Atkin's Court Forms*, 1999, Butterworths, and Jacob, IHJ and Goldrein, I, *Bullen and Leake, Precedents: Principles and Practice*, 1990, Sweet & Maxwell, are also invaluable and comprehensive sources of precedents.

4.1.1 The purpose and significance of statements of case

Statements of case perform a number of important functions: their primary purpose is set out the essentials of your client's case. When drafting a statement of case, always bear in mind the words of CPR 16.6(1): 'Particulars of claim must include (a) a *concise* statement of the facts on which the claimant relies ...'

Secondly, never forget that your statement of case is your first opportunity to make the court or tribunal understand your case. Use them to set out the issues of fact (and, if necessary, law) in a clear and succinct framework and to help yourself to define the issues between the parties when preparing for trial or advising on evidence. RN Hill and J O'Hare recommend that 'a pleading should be bold, blunt and belligerent' (*Civil Litigation*, 1995, FT Law & Tax, p 148).

Finally, statements of case constitute a record of the issues for the purposes of trial and appeal. When settling a statement of case, always remember: you may have to stand up in court and fight a case on the basis of what you have drafted. Do not set out matters which cannot be supported by evidence or legal argument or which are irrelevant.

4.1.2 Matters which must be included

Statements of case are also designed to enable your opponent(s) to appreciate what the issues are in the case and to ensure that they are not taken by surprise. The main principles are that statements of case must state only material facts and must contain sufficient but not excessive detail. Make sure that you specifically include any matter which must be included. These are set out in CPR 16.4 and PD 16. However, the most common matters which must be set out are:

(1) Contributory negligence. In the absence of a plea of contributory negligence, the trial judge is not entitled to make a finding that the claimant's negligence contributed to the accident: *Fookes v Slaytor* [1978] 1 WLR 1293.

(2) Exemplary or aggravated damages.

(3) Fraud. Any allegation of fraud must be pleaded with the utmost particularity and it cannot be pleaded unless there is 'clear and sufficient evidence to support it' (*per* Lord Denning, MR, *Associated Leisure Limited v Associated Newspapers Limited* [1970] 2 QB 450, p 456). Furthermore, r 13.4.2 of the Bar Code of Conduct states that a barrister instructed to settle a pleading may not allege fraud unless:

(a) he has clear instructions to allege fraud; and

(b) he has before him reasonably credible material which, as it stands, establishes a *prima facie* case of fraud.

Improper allegations of fraud may amount to professional misconduct.

(4) Illegality.

(5) Interest (see *Practice Note* [1983] 1 All ER 934).

(6) Want of jurisdiction.

(7) Limitation (see para 2.2, above).

(8) Provisional damages. It is a condition precedent to an award of provisional damages that such a claim has been pleaded (see RSC Ord 37, r 8(1)(a)). The facts relied upon should include those set out in s 32A of the Supreme Court Act 1981 (that is, that there is a chance that at some time in the future the claimant will develop some serious disease or suffer some serious deterioration in his physical or mental condition). The prayer to the claim should also specifically include a claim for provisional damages.

(9) Set off and counterclaim.

(10) The Statute of Frauds or s 2 of the Law of Property (Miscellaneous Provisions) Act 1989.

This list is not exhaustive.

4.1.3 Matters which must not be included

It is equally important that the following matters should not be included:

* an interim payment;

* a Part 36 payment into court (unless the defence of tender before action is being pleaded.

4.1.4 Practical drafting

A well drafted case is essential to the clarification of the issues between the parties. A good statement of case will define and limit the scope of the evidence to be called at trial and will also serve as a useful starting point for a consideration by the parties of the evidence which they will have to call at trial to prove their case.

Well drafted statements of case are good tactical weapons in the litigation battle. Use your statements of case to take and retain the initiative. Keep your opponents working because, whilst they are working on the case, they are expending money and devoting time to litigation. This may at least give them an incentive to settle the case.

Amendments are made in red, then re-amendments in green, then violet, then in yellow.

4.1.5 New terminology

The introduction of the CPR has brought about a considerable number of changes in the preparation of statements of case. Not only has a new language of pleading been introduced, a new approach to drafting statements of case is required.

Some of the established drafting terms have changed.

Old term	New term
Plaintiff	Claimant
Guardian *ad litem* or Next Friend	Litigation Friend
Writ of Summons/County Court Summons	Claim Form
Pleadings	Statements of Case (that is, Claim Form, Particulars of Claim, Defence, Part 20 Claim, Reply to Defence, Further Information)
Statement of Claim/Particulars of Claim	Particulars of Claim
Counterclaim Third Party Proceedings Contribution Proceedings	Part 20 Claim
Requests for Further and Better Particulars/Interrogatories	Requests for Further Information
Discovery	Disclosure

4.1.6 New requirements

The CPR also impose a number of new requirements upon the draftsman.

- Where the claimant is making a claim for money, his claim form must contain a statement of value: CPR 16.3. He must either state:
  - ○ the amount of money he is claiming; or
  - ○ that he expects to recover note more than £5,000, or more than £5,000 but not more than £15,000, or more than £15,000; or
  - ○ he cannot say how much he expects to recover.

  In calculating his likely recovery, a claimant must disregard any possibility that he may recover interest and costs or that a deduction may be made for contributory negligence or to reflect a defence of set off: CPR 16.3(6).

Particular requirements also apply in the case of personal injury claims and claims by tenants of residential property: CPR 16.3(3) and (4).

• All statements of case must also be verified by a *statement of truth*: CPR 22.1(1)(a). For example, particulars of claim would be verified in the following way by a claimant:

'I believe that the facts stated in these particulars of claim are true.'

4.1.7 Stylistic changes

The CPR has also introduced a number of fundamental changes to the approach to be taken when drafting statements of case.

• A more liberal approach to stating evidence, law and documents appears to be evident: see PD 16, para 10.3. It is now provided that particulars of claim may include a reference to a point of law on which the claim is based, the name of any witness whom the claimant intends to call and copies of any documents which the claimant considers is necessary to his claim may be attached (for example, an expert's report).

• The provisions relating to the drafting of defences are, as we shall consider, more onerous and require a defendant who denies an allegation to state his reasons for doing so: CPR 16.5(2).

The clear intention of the new provisions appears to be to focus the parties in preparing their statements of case on:

• the clear identification of the issues between them; and

• the statement of their respective positions on their issues.

4.2   The claim form

All proceedings are now started by a Part 7 claim form (in Form N1) or a Part 8 claim form (in practice form N208). A Part 7 claim form corresponds to the former High Court writ or county court summons procedure, to be used in cases where there are disputed issues of fact. A Part 8 claim form is used where there are no substantial issues of fact and where the claimant seeks the resolution of specific issues or a specific remedy (akin to the former originating summons procedure under the RSC). In this section, we shall consider the requirements of the Part 7 claim form. The procedure regulating these is set out in CPR Pts 7 and 16. The principal features are:

- The claim form must contain a concise statement of the nature of the claim, the remedy the claimant seeks and, where appropriate, a statement of value: CPR 16.2(1). In this form, it resembles generally endorsed writ under the former procedure.
- If the particulars of claim are not contained in the claim form or served with it, then the claimant must state on the claim form that the particulars of claim will follow.
- The claim form must be verified by a statement of truth: CPR 22.1.

It will usually only be appropriate to serve a claim form containing a concise statement of the claim (rather than serving a fully pleaded particulars of claim) in cases where it is anticipated that the claim is straightforward and is unlikely to be defended. In all other cases full particulars of claim should be prepared. Never forget that your particulars of claim are your client's first opportunity to present his case most attractively to the judge. It is likely to be the first document that he will read. Never pass up the opportunity of setting out the material facts, evidence and law to your client's best advantage. Use your statements of case to frame the issues in the way best suited to your client's case.

4.3 The particulars of claim

The principal purpose of the particulars of claim is to set out your client's case as clearly and succinctly as possible. CPR 16.4 and PD 16 set out the matters which must be included in particulars of claim. In addition to those matters mentioned earlier, the new Rules also make new provisions in a number of material respects:

- where a claim is based upon a *written agreement,* a copy of the contract or documents constituting the agreement should be attached to or served with the particulars of claim and the original(s) should be available at the hearing of the action: PD 16, para 10.3. In addition, any general conditions of sale incorporated into a contract should also be attached. If the contractual documents or terms are bulky, only relevant extracts need to be attached;
- where a claim is based upon an *oral agreement,* the particulars of claim should set out the contractual words used and state by whom, to whom, when and where they were spoken: PD 16, para 10.4;
- where an agreement is based on *conduct,* the conduct relied upon must be specified and the persons involved, place and date of the acts relied upon stated: PD 16, para 10.5;

- as indicated earlier, PD 16 sets out lists of specific matters which must be included in claims in respect of personal injuries, fatal accidents, the recovery of land, hire purchase or defamation.

4.3.1 Drafting the particulars of claim

Before you draft anything, you must have a grasp of the facts material to the causes of action which you are going to allege. It is good practice to proceed as follows:

(1) Write down the causes of action which you are going to allege, for example, breach of contract, negligence, nuisance.

(2) Write down the essential facts which underlie each cause of action, for example:

    (a) Breach of contract:

        (i)   the parties;

        (ii)   the agreement;

        (iii)   the essential terms;

        (iv)   the nature of the alleged breach;

        (v)   the nature, cause and extent of the loss and damage or other relief claimed.

    (b) Negligence:

        (i)   the parties;

        (ii)   the material facts giving rise to the duty of care;

        (iii)   the breach of the duty of care;

        (iv)   the nature, cause and extent of the loss and damage; and

        (v)   the relief claimed.

    (c) Nuisance:

        (i)   the parties;

        (ii)   the nature of the claimant's interest in the relevant property;

        (iii)   the nature, cause and extent of the nuisance;

        (iv)   the nature, cause and extent of the loss and damage; and

        (v)   the relief claimed.

(3) If you do not know what material facts you should be setting out, look at a precedent and analyse the purpose of each of its paragraphs to establish what that draftsman thought was necessary. It is only when you know what facts you must plead that you can appreciate whether you have derived all the relevant information from the

client. If you have not, don't avoid the issue: establish the missing details from the client.

(4) Use the framework of the material facts of the cause of action to structure the paragraphs of your draft. As far as possible, set out one allegation per paragraph. Subdivide your paragraphs if necessary. A long series of carefully worded sub-paragraphs may have the effect of making your case seem stronger than it is.

(5) Keep your sentences short.

(6) Consider every word and phrase you use and weigh up their value. Ask yourself whether each is necessary and what each adds to the case.

(7) Limit your allegations to those which you are confident you can prove. Avoid exaggeration.

(8) Do not be afraid to allege alternatives.

(9) As far as possible, set out events in strict chronological order.

(10) Always refer to the same person or thing in the same way throughout the pleading. In long or complicated cases, draft a paragraph defining the relevant people and terms at the start of the pleading.

(11) Do not anticipate potential defences unless there are very good tactical reasons for doing so.

4.3.2 Particular drafting problems

Setting out contracts

You should set out an alleged agreement as fully as possible. In a written agreement:

> By a written agreement dated 25 July 1999 and signed by John Smith on behalf of the claimant and David Jones on behalf of the defendant ... A copy of that agreement is produced as Annex A to this document ...

or

> By a written agreement contained in an exchange of correspondence between the claimant and the defendant as particularised below it was agreed that ... Copies of those letters are produced as Annex A to this document.

Particulars

(a) A letter dated 1 July 1999 from the claimant to the defendant.

(b) A letter dated 4 July 1999 from the defendant to the claimant.

(c) A letter dated 5 July 1999 from the claimant to the defendant.

If the agreement is partly oral and partly in writing:

> By an agreement made partly orally during a meeting between the claimant and the defendant on 21 April 1999 at the claimant's offices and partly in writing by a letter dated 26 April 1999 from the claimant to the defendant ...

If it is an oral agreement:

> By an oral agreement made between the claimant and the defendant in the course of a telephone conversation on 18 February 1999 ... [set out the gist of the conversation]

or an oral agreement evidenced in writing:

> By an oral agreement made between the claimant and the defendant at a meeting at the claimant's office at 10 Smith Street, London SE4 on 26 October 1999 and evidenced in writing by a letter dated 27 October 1999 from the defendant to the claimant ...

Particulars of injuries. Particulars of injuries should be pleaded as fully as possible. This may promote an advantageous settlement. Remember that the judge will form his initial view as to the seriousness of your client's injuries from the particulars. Do your case justice from the outset. In a personal injuries case, not only should details of the claimant's injuries be set out, his date of birth and a schedule of his past and future losses should be included, together with a copy of any medical report to be relied upon: PD 16, para 4.1 to 4.4.

Particulars of negligence. Always take the trouble to analyse the negligent acts or omissions into their component parts and establish precisely what the defendant did or failed to do which rendered his acts or omissions negligent. Consider the possible allegations of negligence in the most basic motor car accident. These are normally that the defendant was negligent in that he:

- drove too fast;

- failed to observe or heed the presence of the claimant in the road;

- failed to give priority to the claimant and/or failed to heed traffic signs;

- failed to give any or any adequate warning of his presence in the road, in particular by sounding his horn or flashing his headlights;
- failed to brake adequately or at all;
- failed to swerve, steer or otherwise manage or control the motor car so as to avoid colliding with the claimant;
- failed to stop;
- hit the claimant.

Foreign currency

If the claimant seeks judgment in a currency other than pounds sterling, this should be expressly stated in the claim form. The particulars of claim must also expressly state:

(1) the claim is for payment in a specified foreign currency;

(2) why the claim is made for payment in that currency;

(3) the sterling equivalent of the sum at the date of the claim; and

(4) the source of the exchange rate relied on.

Pleading documents

If certain documents will be referred to at trial, state as follows: 'The claimant will refer at trial to [that letter] for its full terms, true meaning and effect.' Don't forget, relevant documents can now be annexed to the statement of case.

Implication of terms

A common form of words used to plead the implication of a contractual term is: 'The term is to be implied into the Agreement to give business efficacy to it and/or to give effect to the true intention of the parties.'

4.4 The defence

The functions of the defence principally are:

(1) to set out all the material facts disclosing the defence;

(2) to define and restrict the issues between the parties. It is a waste of time and money to prolong 'issues' which are not in dispute. In drafting the defence, therefore, you should aim to:

    (a) state what parts of the particulars of claim the defendant admits; and

(b) state what parts of the particulars of claim he denies; and

(3) to raise all the issues necessary to establish the defence and to comply with CPR 16.5 and PD 16, paras 15.1 to 17.

4.4.1 Drafting the defence and counterclaim

The guidelines set out in para 4.2.1 are equally applicable to drafting a defence. However, a number of additional pointers are also helpful. First, before you do anything else, carefully read the particulars of claim in order to:

- see whether it discloses a cause of action and exactly how many (and what) causes of action;

- ascertain whether or not the claim is, or parts of it are, time barred;

- establish precisely what are the material facts of the claim;

- generally see upon what basis the claimant is claiming.

If the claimant has served a 'short form' claim form, plead the defendant's case as fully as possible. The detailed version of events contained in the defence will, therefore, be the first to be read by the judge at trial, unless the claimant amends his particulars of claim. Never pass up the opportunity of putting your case most attractively before the judge.

If your client's defence has little substance to it, you may wish to 'flesh it out' by:

(1) pleading to the particulars of claim in as full a manner as possible;

(2) not simply denying (or making no admissions to) allegations simply by reference to the paragraph number, that is, 'Paragraph 4 of the particulars of claim is denied'. If it is appropriate, repeat the allegation and deny or make no admissions to it;

(3) setting out as many material facts as possible (whilst keeping it relevant);

(4) considering whether there is any conceivable set off or counterclaim which could be raised in relation to this claim or arising out of any other transactions. A set off is a monetary cross claim which is also a defence to the claim made by the claimant. A counterclaim is a separate claim which does not, of itself, amount to a defence to the claimant's claim.

These steps should lead to a document which has some physical substance, at least, if little real content. Even a weak defence may be enough either to avoid summary judgment proceedings or to establish a starting point for reducing the amount of the claimant's claim in settlement negotiations.

The most important rule in drafting a defence is to ensure that every material allegation in the particulars of claim has been responded to. There are basically three ways of dealing with an allegation:

(1) To admit it. If admissions are made, ensure that they are limited in their scope to guarantee that nothing is inadvertently admitted. Check that admissions made will not have an adverse effect on your client outside of the particular proceedings. Take great care if you are admitting entire paragraphs. Break up the paragraph which you intend to admit and analyse the allegations made to ensure each one can properly be admitted. Read and re-read the paragraph in the particulars of claim to ensure that there are no 'hidden' allegations which are being admitted. Only admit causation of damage, and loss and damage in rare circumstances. Once an allegation is admitted, it ceases to be an issue in the action.

(2) To deny it. It is appropriate to deny an allegation if it is disputed and you have evidence to lead in support of the denial. In these circumstances the defendant should deny the allegation and then proceed to put forward its own positive version of events. CPR 16.5(2) provides that, where the defendant denies an allegation, he must state his reasons for doing so and, if he intends to put forward a different version of events, he *must* state his own version. If a defendant intends to advance a positive case in relation to mitigation loss and damage, that must also be set out.

(3) To 'not admit' it. It is appropriate to 'make no admissions' as to an allegation or to 'not admit' it if the defendant has no positive case to put forward with regard to that allegation and is simply putting the claimant to proof of it. It is usual, for example, to make no admissions as to the loss and damage allegedly sustained by a claimant. CPR 16.5(1) indicates it is appropriate to 'not admit' matters if the defendant is *unable* to adopt or deny them.

If a defendant has set up in his defence, the nature of his case in relation to an issue to which a particular allegation is relevant but fails specifically to deal with it, he is to be taken as requiring it to be proved: CPR 16.5(3). In other cases, if a defendant *fails* to deal with an allegation, he is to be taken to admit it: CPR 16.5(5). It is *essential*, therefore, to ensure that every allegation is properly addressed.

Prior to the implementation of the CPR, it was common for pleadings to contain what was called the 'general traverse' as a 'sweep up', that is, a paragraph containing the following (or a similar) form of words: 'All allegations made in the Statement of Claim which have not been expressly admitted or not admitted above are repeated here and specifically denied.'

This was something of a legal 'safety net' to ensure that all allegations have been dealt with. It may still be appropriate to use it at the end of a defence to a long and/or complicated particulars of claim or Part 20 claim but it should never be considered sufficient for dealing with central allegations. Always make sure that you deal in the defence with all the material allegations which have been made in the particulars of claim. If necessary, make a checklist of each of the allegations made and ensure that you know how you have pleaded to each of them. Don't fudge issues. Make sure that you have clear instructions from your client and that you put his, or its, case clearly and accurately. He may have to give evidence in support of your particulars of claim.

Always consider whether it is appropriate to settle a request for further information.

4.4.2 Approaches to drafting

There are a variety of approaches to the actual drafting of the defence. The appropriate method in any particular case depends upon a number of factors, principally the way in which the particulars of claim have been pleaded and the strength of the defendant's case.

If the particulars of claim are in short form or are poorly drafted in that they are illogical, convoluted or over particularised, it is advisable to draft the defence as one would formulate a full particulars of claim setting out in full the defendant's version of events and then specifically addressing the material allegations contained in the particulars of claim. If, however, the particulars of claim is properly drafted and clear and concise, a useful approach is to examine each issue in detail and consider each allegation made and the defendant's response to it. Paragraphs can then be pleaded to as follows:

> Save that it is admitted that ... and save that no admissions are made as to ... paragraph 1 of the particulars of claim is denied.

The defendant can then make any positive allegations of fact to ground its defence or counterclaim, these should be woven into the pleading where appropriate.

When the defendant also has a counterclaim, it is important to ensure that the facts and matters necessary to establish the cause of action relied upon are fully set out in either the defence or the counterclaim. If they are set out in the defence, they can simply be incorporated by formally repeating the appropriate paragraphs in the first paragraph of the counterclaim in the following way: 'The defendant repeats paragraphs 1–5 and 7–9 of its defence.' The counterclaim is then drafted as you would draft particulars of claim save that it is not necessary to repeat again the allegations made in the defence which are relied upon. The prayer to the counterclaim begins: 'AND the defendant counterclaims: …'

4.4.3 Counterclaims against additional parties

The defendant need not counterclaim only against the claimant, but may also include relief against other persons not already parties to the claim between the claimant and himself. CPR 20.5 deals with the circumstances in which a counterclaim may be made against additional parties. The defendant must, in such circumstances, apply to the court for an order that the other person be joined as a defendant to the counterclaim. The procedure for such an application is set out in PD 20, paras 1 and 2.

Remember: Both a defence and a Part 20 claim *must* be verified by a statement of truth.

4.5   The reply

The service of a reply is now, effectively, optional. If one is to be served, its functions are to limit the issues between the parties by admitting such of the defendant's case as can properly be admitted and to raise any issues which must be specifically raised to prevent the defendant being taken by surprise, for example, fraud, limitation, any fact showing illegality or which tends to make any claim or defence raised by the defendant untenable. A reply can also be used to plead any new facts which the claimant can prove to defeat a defence put forward by the defendant.

If no reply is served, the claimant is *not* taken to admit the matters raised in the defence: CPR 16.7(1). In these circumstances, if the only function of a reply would be to join issue with the defendant, then it is worth considering very seriously whether its service is necessary, since the costs of preparing and serving it may be disallowed.

4.5.1 Drafting the reply and defence to counterclaim

The defence to counterclaim is drafted on the same basis as any other defence (see paras 4.3.1 and 4.3.2). When drafting the reply, bear the following points in mind:

- Look through the defence for the points with which you agree and ensure that they are admitted in the reply.

- Analyse your case and consider whether there are any matters which must be specifically pleaded.

- Ensure that you lay the groundwork for any material allegations which you wish to rely upon in the defence to counterclaim.

- Remember that you cannot rectify a defective particulars of claim by supplementing it with material pleaded in the reply. If your particulars of claim are defective, amend them: PD 16, para 12.2.

- You should divide the reply and defence to counterclaim into two separate parts, one headed, 'Reply' and the other 'Defence to counterclaim', but number their paragraphs sequentially throughout.

4.6   Pleadings subsequent to the reply

No party may file or serve any statement of case after a reply without the court's permission.

4.7   Requests for further information

A well drafted request for further information can be a powerful weapon in the litigation battle. Such requests can be used to force your opponent to disclose more of his case than he might wish (or than he is able to). They may be used to embarrass overstated claims and are useful in forcing the other side to restrict their claims, or at times even to withdraw them.

Draftsmen tend to gloss over the weaker aspects of their case or the matters on which they have not been able to obtain detailed instructions. Learn to scour every statement of case you receive to identify the other side's weak points and to probe it with a request.

CPR 18 and PD 18 – *Further Information* – detail the procedure to be followed in making requests for further information. CPR 18.1 provides that the court may, at any time, order a party to clarify any matter which is in dispute in the proceedings or give additional information in relation to such matters, *whether or not the matter is contained or referred to in a statement of case.*

The power under the new Rules to request information is, therefore, considerably broader than the former power under the RSC and CCR to request further and better particulars of a pleading. The request does not have to be tied to the wording of a statement of case and the new powers can be used to force a party plainly to state the factual basis of its case and, for example, to set out its positive case in relation to any matters which it has denied. It is also significant that responses to requests for information have to be verified by a statement of truth: CPR 22.1.

PD 18, para 1 provides that, before a party may apply for an order requiring another party to supply further clarification or information, it must first serve on the other party a written request. That request for information or clarification should:

- state a date by which a response is to be served. That date must afford the answering party a reasonable time to respond;
- be concise and strictly confined to matters which are reasonably necessary and proportionate to enable the requesting party to prepare his own case or to understand the case he has to meet;
- identify itself as a request under Pt 18;
- comply with the formal requirements of PD 18, para 1.5.

4.7.1 Practical points

When drafting your requests, ensure that:

- each request is numbered;
- the paragraph or sub-paragraph of the statement of case of which particulars are sought is identified by its number and/or letter if the request relates to a party's pleaded case;
- the words of which particulars are sought are set out;
- you limit your requests for clarification or for information which is reasonably necessary and proportionate to enable you to prepare your client's case or to understand the case he has to meet.

Always take great care in drafting your request. Think what you are trying to elicit. Try and cover every conceivable eventuality. Do not let your opponent escape because of sloppy drafting on your part.

It is also beneficial to try and keep your individual requests as short and specific as possible by dividing a large request up into its constituent parts. This forces the opposition to give specific answers and enables you to identify the areas of weakness in their case.

You should seek to avoid the other side gaining an order for further information against your client. If an order is made that a request for further information be answered, it is not possible to refuse to answer the request, even though it may be an improper request (see *Fearis v Davies* [1989] FSR 555). If an application is made for an order, ensure that your client is represented at the hearing to prevent an order being made for requests which should not have been sought.

Make sure that when you receive the information or clarification you have requested that your opponent has fully answered your requests and is not avoiding the difficult questions. If he is, apply to the court for an order that the information be provided.

4.7.2 Two examples of a general purpose request

Two areas where pleaders are particularly lax in their drafting, and which are often crucial to a party's case, are the formation and existence of a contract (and its terms) and the claim for loss and damage. CPR 16.4 and PD 16, para 10 emphasise the importance of setting out such matters and, consequently, if they have been inadequately pleaded, seek clarification.

Example 1

Under paragraph 1

Of: 'By an agreement made between the Claimant and the Defendant ...'

Request

(1) Please state whether the agreement was made orally or in writing or partly orally and partly in writing.

(2) Insofar as in writing, please identify with full and proper particularity each and every document relied upon and produce a copy of it pursuant to CPR Pt 31.14.

(3) Insofar as made orally, please identify by whom on behalf of the claimant the agreement was made, with whom on behalf of the defendant, when, where and upon what occasion and give the gist of the words used in so agreeing.

(4) Please identify each and every item of the agreement which the claimant relies upon, stating in each case whether the term is an express or an implied term.

(5) In the case of each and every express term identified under the reply to (4) above, state whether it was expressly agreed orally or in writing.

(6) Insofar as in writing, please identify with full and proper particularity each and every document relied upon and produce a copy of it pursuant to CPR Pt 31.14.

(7) Insofar as agreed orally, please identify by whom on behalf of the claimant and with whom each and every term was allegedly agreed when, where and upon what occasion and give the gist of the words used in so agreeing.

(8) In the case of each and every term which it is alleged was to be implied into the agreement, please state whether it is alleged that it was to be implied:

(a) by law; or

(b) upon some other basis.

(9) If the reply to (8) above is that the term is to be implied by law, please identify the provision relied upon.

(10) If the reply to (8) above is that the term is implied upon some other basis, please identify the basis relied upon and state with full and proper particularity all material averments necessary to establish the alleged basis of the implication.

Note: The defendant expects a Response to this request for information/clarification by 26 September 1999.

Example 2

Under paragraph 7

Of: 'The claimant has suffered loss and damage in the sum of £10,989.54 in respect of the cost of remedial works carried out by the claimant. Further the claimant has been put to anxiety, inconvenience and distress.'

Request

(1) Please state with full and proper particularity how that figure is calculated or arrived at.

(2) Without prejudice to the generality of the foregoing, please identify with full and proper particularity what part of that sum is attributable to:

(a)   labour charges;

(b)   materials; and

(c)   other items.

(3) In respect of such part of the sum as is attributable to labour, please identify with full and proper particularity:

(a)   each and every person in respect of whose time charge is made;

(b)   the rate of charge in respect of each person identified under (a) above and how the same is calculated or arrived at; and

(c)   the dates and hours of work carried out on each of those dates by each of the persons identified under (a) above.

(4) In respect of such part of the sum as is attributable to materials, please identify each and every item in respect of which claim is made, the date it was acquired, from whom and at what price.

(5) In respect of such part of the sum as is attributable to other items, please state what items are claimed and provide full and proper particulars of the claim.

(6) Please provide full and proper particulars of each occasions upon which the claimant relies when it is alleged that the claimant suffered anxiety, inconvenience, or distress and provide full and proper particulars of the complaint made in each case.

Note: The defendant expects a Response to this request for information/clarification by 10 June 1999.

5 Witness Statements and Affidavits

5.1 Introduction

Witness statements and affidavits are the form in which evidence is most commonly presented for the purposes of interim applications. Prior to the implementation of the CPR, the usual way of adducing evidence in pre-trial applications was by way of affidavit. The CPR effected a change. The usual rule that now applies is that evidence at such hearings will be in the form of a witness statement unless the court otherwise directs or the Rules or statute expressly provide for evidence by way of affidavit: CPR 32.6(1). Furthermore, evidence in support of the following applications must also be given by affidavit:

- a search order (formerly an *Anton Piller* order);
- a freezing injunction (previously called a *Mareva* injunction);
- an order requiring an occupier to permit another to enter on his land;
- an order against anyone who is alleged to be in contempt of court (CPR PD 32, para 1.4).

Witness statements are also the most common means by which a witness's primary evidence is adduced in chief at trial. A well drafted witness statement or affidavit is, therefore, a useful means of presenting your client's case in a persuasive and coherent manner before the court. In this chapter, the basic procedural rules relating to witness statements and affidavits and their uses, as well as the technique of drafting such documents will be considered.

5.2   Formal requirements of witness statements

A witness statement is simply a written statement verified by a statement of truth setting out in numbered paragraphs the evidence of the maker of the statement. CPR 32.8 provides that a witness statement must comply with the requirements of PD 32, paras 17–22. Reference should be made to these provisions for the detail of what is required. The principal matters to remember, however, are:

- The witness statement should be headed with the name and action number of the proceedings. At the top right hand corner of the first page there should clearly be written:

  (1) the party on whose behalf it is made;

  (2) the initials and surname of the witness;

  (3) the number of the statement in relation to that witness;

  (4) the identifying initials and number of each exhibit referred to; and

  (5) the date the statement was made.

  See the example set out on the next page

- The witness statement must, if practicable, be in the intended witness's own words and should state:

  ○ his full name;

  ○ his place of residence or business address (if he is giving evidence in a professional capacity);

  ○ his occupation; and

  ○ the fact that he is a party to the proceedings or an employee of a party to the proceedings (if that be the case).

- The witness statement must identify which parts of the witness's evidence are within his own knowledge and which parts are matters of information or belief.

- All numbers, including dates, should be expressed in figures, for example, 23 May 2000.

- The witness statement must be verified by a statement of truth.

Example

(1) Claimant

(2) A McBeal

(3) 1st

(4) A McB 1

(5) 30 June 1999

1999 I No 922

IN THE HIGH COURT OF JUSTICE

QUEEN'S BENCH DIVISION

BETWEEN:

DAVID BRIXEN

Claimant

–and–

PETER MORTER

Defendant

1st WITNESS STATEMENT OF ALISON McBEAL

Background

1. I am Alison McBeal of McBeal & Co, Solicitors of North Street, London WC1Y 9RY. I am a Partner in the firm of McBeal & Co. and have conduct of this Action on behalf of the Claimant, Mr Brixen.

2. I make this witness statement in support of Mr Brixen's applications for summary judgment for damages to be assessed under CPR Part 24 and for an interim payment under CPR Part 25. Unless indicated to the contrary, the matters with which I deal in this statement are within my own knowledge. Where they are not, I shall identify the sources of any information or belief upon which I rely.

3. I produce with this statement a paginated bundle of documents identified as A McB 1. References in this statement in square brackets are references to the corresponding pages of that bundle of documents.

4. The application for summary judgment is made under CPR Part 24 because Mr Brixen believes that on the evidence the Defendant, Mr Morter, has no real prospect of successfully defending the claim and Mr Brixen knows of no other reason why the disposal of the claim against him should await trial. The contents of the Particulars of Claim in this Action are true. In this statement I shall adopt the definitions used in it.

....

STATEMENT OF TRUTH

I believe that the facts stated in this witness statement are true.

Signed

ALISON McBEAL

Partner, McBeal & Co

Solicitor to the Claimant

Date

5.3   Formal requirements of affidavits

An affidavit is simply a written statement of evidence sworn (or affirmed) by its maker, the deponent, before a person authorised to make affidavits which, subject to the rules of court, is admissible in evidence in legal proceedings. An affidavit cannot be sworn before a person in a firm of solicitors which is acting for a party in the dispute. Although the general rule (subject to the exceptions identified earlier) is that evidence in interim proceedings is adduced by witness statement, nothing in the CPR prevents a witness from giving evidence by affidavit, but the additional costs of making the affidavit may not be recovered unless the court orders otherwise: CPR 32.15(2).

CPR 32.16 provides that an affidavit must comply with the requirements of PD 32, paras 2-16. Reference should be made to these provisions for the detail of what is required. The principal matters to remember, however, are:

(1) The affidavit should be given the title of the cause or matter in which it will be used.

(2) Every affidavit must be expressed in the first person and, unless the court directs otherwise, must state:

(a) the deponent's place of residence unless evidence is given in a business capacity in which case his business address, his position and the name of his firm or employer must be given;

(b) his occupation or, if he has none, his description; and

(c) if he is employed by a party to the cause or matter, this must be disclosed.

(3) Every affidavit must be bound in book form and the pages numbered consecutively.

(4) Every affidavit must be divided into consecutively numbered paragraphs, each paragraph as far as possible being confined to a distinct issue.

(5) Dates, sums and numbers must be expressed in figures, not words.

(6) Every affidavit, including those by the solicitor or the senior clerks of the county court or High Court administering the oath, must be signed by the deponent and the jurat. Details of when, where and witnesses must be completed and signed by the person before whom it is sworn.

Remember that, in the case of application made without notice, the affidavit must make full and frank disclosure of all matters relevant to the case. In the event of hearsay evidence being used, it is important to state the source of the information being used.

Copies of individual letters should not be made separate exhibits. They should be collected together and exhibited as a bundle or bundles, arranged in chronological order and paginated in the centre at the bottom of the page. Where a deponent deposes in a single action to more than one affidavit to which there are exhibits, the numbering of the exhibits should run consecutively throughout and not begin again with each affidavit.

5.4 Drafting witness statements and affidavits

5.4.1 Considerations

Given the large number of proceedings in which witness statements and affidavits can be used and the wide variety of drafting styles it is impossible to lay down hard and fast rules governing their drafting. A number of fundamental principles should, however, always be borne in mind.

Before you start drafting, consider the purpose for which the evidence is being adduced and the nature of the application in which it is intended to be used. It is useful to have the second paragraph of a witness statement or affidavit set out exactly what the purpose of the document is: 'I make this affidavit in support of the plaintiff's application for X ...' In a lengthy case, it makes identification of affidavits and witness statements considerably easier, and lets the reader know what to expect. Make sure that you are aware of all the formal requirements which must be complied with in relation to the particular application. If necessary, make a list of the essential matters and tick them off when they have been dealt with. Also, make a list of both the aims which you wish to achieve in drafting the document, and the issues which have to be dealt with. Be meticulous and systematic and ensure that everything that must be said is said in a structured and coherent way. It may be appropriate to provide a chronology in the affidavit or witness statement.

Bear in mind who is going to read it and what they will know already. If they know nothing of the material facts of the case, set them out in a clear and easily digestible format. This will be particularly important on an application made without notice where the judge will know nothing of the case, but will expect to be able to pick up the facts very quickly. As far as possible, make each affidavit or witness statement a self-contained narrative, and avoid too much cross-referencing. Consider the words you use with care. Express yourself clearly and succinctly. Ask yourself whether each particular sentence is necessary and what it adds to the document as a whole.

As far as possible, keep your sentences short and confine each paragraph to one issue. If necessary, subdivide paragraphs. If you do this, the document should be punchy and direct. This will give it more impact. Don't be afraid to use paragraph headings if they will assist the reader by signposting where the evidence is going and directing his mind to the issues.

Be relevant: don't ramble. If you insert a wedge of irrelevant material into your draft, there is a danger that the reader will skip over it, and in so doing may miss other (relevant) points.

Emphasise your strong points by placing them in separate paragraphs. This avoids them being lost amongst other material.

Do not use florid or intemperate language (even if the deponent or witness might wish to). The court may order a scandalous or irrelevant matter to be struck out although this rarely occurs in practice. In any event, a poorly drafted document will do your client's case more harm than good.

Remember that, ultimately, someone may have to swear the affidavit as their evidence or verify it with a statement of truth. Check that it accurately reflects what they want to say. The witness might have to justify every word under cross-examination at trial. Never draft anything without express instructions or without ensuring that instructions will be taken which cover the precise point. It is not the draftsman's job to 'create' evidence by conjecture to supplement the defects of his client's case.

Whenever possible, check that what you have drafted does not conflict with any previous affidavits or witness statement the witness may have produced or your client's other evidence or statements of case. If it does, seek instructions as to the reasons for the disparity and, if necessary, re-draft the document to take account of any fresh instructions. When you have a final draft, read it and re-read it to check that it complies with all appropriate rules and, equally importantly, that it reads well. If you find the resulting draft to be tedious, it is likely that the reader will too. Remember that it is always easier to read an interesting document than a tedious one. The more readable the evidence, the more the reader will absorb of your case. In a complex case, you may wish to 'tell the story' through one 'lead affidavit' or witness statement with other witnesses referring to it or merely confirming its accuracy. Often, an affidavit or witness statement from the witness himself is likely to have more impact than one sworn or verified by a solicitor on the basis of his instructions. Never forget that this is your opportunity to convince the reader of the strength of your client's case: don't waste it.

Occasionally, it is necessary in an affidavit or witness statement not simply to lay the facts before the court but also to submit arguments to it or to invite it to draw conclusions favourable to your client from the evidence adduced. Do this carefully, but do not be afraid of urging with force your client's contentions. This may be appropriate at the start or, more usually, at the conclusion of the document.

In the event of your opponent contending successfully that your client's affidavit or witness statement is defective, remember the provisions of CPR 25.2, which permit irregular affidavits and witness statements to be filed with the leave of the judge. If your affidavit or witness statement is defective, seek leave to have the same admitted as evidence notwithstanding the defect.

6 Settlement

6.1 General points

It is often more difficult to settle cases than to fight them. Ensure that any settlement covers all issues, as you will not get a second bite of the cherry and it is not possible to appeal. A faulty or ill considered settlement may lead to more litigation. Settlements may be made by letter, round table agreement, or by accepting money paid into court. Before the action reaches a hearing, proceedings may be stayed, discontinued or adjourned on terms agreed. Too often, settlements are reached only at the doors of the court/tribunal. Then, they may be endorsed on the lawyers' 'briefs' or form a consent order made by the judge.

The settlement may need to be enforced by further litigation, so make sure you tie up all loose ends, especially any costs orders already made before the case reaches that stage. You may agree that there will be 'liberty to apply' but, if so, ensure that the scope of such liberty is clearly stated. They will normally allow the matter to be restored only in the case of difficulties about the meaning or enforcement of an order (see *Practice Direction* [1980] 1 All ER 1008; *Chanel v FW Woolworth* [1981] 1 All ER 745).

Solicitors do have ostensible authority to settle cases, but ensure that the client is aware of what is being agreed in his name. Interim applications for injunctions are often settled on undertakings being given to the court; in this case they are enforceable by contempt proceedings to the same extent as if an order was made by the court itself.

Settlements can only be challenged by the parties in the same circumstances in which ordinary contracts can be avoided, for example, fraud, undue influence, mistake or misrepresentation (see *Huddersfield Banking Co Ltd v Henry Lister & Son Ltd* [1895] 2 Ch 273). In many jurisdictions (for example, employment tribunals and the Family Division), there are conventional methods of achieving settlements. For further information, see Foskett, D, *The Law and Practice of Compromise*, 1996, Sweet & Maxwell and Foskett, D, *Settlement Under the Civil Procedure Rules*, 1999, Sweet & Maxwell.

6.2   Tomlin order

The most common form of settlement in the civil courts is the 'Tomlin order' which commonly reads as follows:

> And the claimant and defendant having agreed to the terms set forth in the schedule hereto, it is ordered that all further proceedings in this action be stayed except for the purpose of carrying such terms into effect. Liberty to apply as to carrying such terms into effect.

A revised form of this order ('The new millennium Tomlin order') can be found in *Settlement Under the Civil Procedure Rules,* p 110.

7 Advocacy

7.1 Before attending court

7.1.1 Lists of authorities

You should telephone, write or fax to your opponent and the court a list of the cases on which you intend to rely in the case. Usually, this is done the night before or the morning of the case. In general, the onus is on the claimant or appellant to send his or her list first. Use the official law reports (that is, AC, QB, Ch, ICR) when a case is reported in those reports, and the Weekly Law Reports, All England Reports or specialist reports only when it is not so reported. Hand in a legible list of authorities to the court usher in good time before the hearing. If possible, provide an indexed photocopied bundle of authorities.

7.1.2 Adjourning cases

Do not apply at the last minute to the court or tribunal for an adjournment. In the High Court, all such applications go before a single judge appointed for the purpose, and applications are rarely considered favourably when a 'fixture' has been given for a case. It is always important to give full reasons for any request for an adjournment (preferably supported by a witness statement).

7.1.3 Correct attire

Barristers must wear wig, gown and bands when appearing in the county court, Crown Court, High Court, Court of Appeal and House of Lords. When appearing in chambers, suits and dresses should be black, dark blue or grey. Solicitors only wear gowns and bands in the county and Crown Courts. A frequent source of confusion for the young practitioner relates to the appropriate dress in county court proceedings for domestic violence. Such an application for an injunction is always heard in chambers and thus no robes are necessary; however, the application to commit a contemnor to prison for breach of an injunction is always heard in open court, and, accordingly, wig and gown is required. If in doubt, always take your robes.

7.1.4 Other preparation

Unless otherwise provided, court bundles should be lodged at least two clear days before the hearing of an application or trial.

Not less than three clear days before the hearing of an action or application, each party should lodge with the court (with copies to other parties) a skeleton argument setting out the party's submissions in respect of each issue.

7.2 Checklist on attending court

(1) Ensure that your case is listed and that you reach the court in good time for the hearing. *The New Court Guide*, 1998, Blackstone, published annually, is an invaluable tool in this respect as it includes the tube, train and bus routes to each court and tribunal in the London area as well as restaurants close to the court.

(2) Ensure that the client has seen the statements of case and relevant documentation and understands the central issues in the case.

(3) Make sure that the witnesses have seen their witness statements and check whether there are any last minute corrections (hopefully not too drastic in scope).

(4) Find out whether the witnesses wish to be sworn or to affirm and let the usher know.

(5) Check whether any witness requires an interpreter. (Ideally this should have been done well in advance of the trial.)

(6) Locate your opponent and discuss with him cases to be cited and any other relevant issues: this is often a good time to float proposals for settlement.

(7) Take notes. You must maintain a good note of evidence given in any hearing, and the blue A4 counsel's notebooks are very useful for this task. Everyone has his or her own likes and dislikes as to note taking, and you will develop your own style over time. The following hints may be of use:

(a)   at the start of each book, make an index recording the witnesses and the times of court sitting;

(b)   write the questions and answers in different colour ink;

(c)   leave the left hand page for your notes and comments; this can cut down time in preparing the closing speech or in cross-examination of a subsequent witness;

(d)   word processors are very useful for recording important evidence day by day and in a long case preparing a potential closing speech. It is very useful to marshall your thoughts in a long case each evening.

(8) Check which side of the court to sit on. In the following courts and tribunals, seating is as follows (looking from the back of the court towards the Judge/bench/tribunal):

(a)   county court: plaintiff on the left, defendant on the right;

(b)   Crown Court: prosecution furthest from the jury box, defence nearest to it;

(c)   Employment Appeal Tribunal: appellant on right, respondent on left;

(d)   High Court: plaintiff on left, defendant on right;

(e)   Employment Tribunal: employer sits on left, employee on right.

(9) On entering the court, bow to whomever is presiding over the court.

(10) Whenever someone is taking the oath or affirming, you should stop talking and ensure that your witnesses do the same.

(11) Make sure that if you are junior counsel, you do not sit in the front row reserved for Queen's Counsel.

(12) If the judge is sitting in open court and your case has concluded, do not leave court until the judge has risen, unless he/she invites you to do so. It is bad etiquette to leave a robed judge sitting in court without any parties present. Wait for the parties in the next case to come in before leaving.

7.3 Courtroom presentation

7.3.1 Introduction

Begin by introducing all the parties to the court, together with the advocate appearing for them. Choose your words carefully, avoiding slang and trying to keep the interest of your audience whoever or whatever they may be.

7.3.2 Authorities

Choose the cases to which you refer with care. State a proposition first and if the judge is prepared to accept it without more ado, merely refer to the name of a case in support. If, however, the judge expresses puzzlement or alarm, take him to the headnote of the case and then any relevant (but only relevant) passage(s). Do not refer to the whole judgment unless it is absolutely necessary. In cases in which more than one judgment has been given, you must refer to all the judgments to indicate the extent with which each judge agrees or disagrees with the submission for which you are using the case. Always be fair in the way in which you cite case law: whenever possible cite from the law reports first (QB, Ch, AC) rather than the law reports published by publishers (other than the Incorporated Council of Law Reporting).

7.3.3 Other points

It is useful to observe other points concerning presentation:

(1) Do not raise your voice in court.

(2) Do not give evidence yourself.

(3) Keep any objections to the conduct of the other party to a minimum; to do otherwise may indicate that you are not very confident of your own case and you may make a mistake in due course on which your opponent will then 'pounce'.

(4) Remember to ask for witnesses to be 'released' after they have given evidence; unless there is any real likelihood that they will be required further to give evidence, they will normally be so released.

(5) Make sure that your questions are formulated as questions and not as statements or opinions. Keep your questions short and simple.

(6) If you have forgotten to ask a specific question of a witness, ask the judge for leave to recall a witness but do not do so unless it is very important to your case, as it may irritate the judge.

(7) Remember that every time you ask a question, you take a risk.

(8) Remember that the witness may be terrified of giving evidence and it is not part of your task to terrify him or her further.

(9) Know your way around your bundle like the back of your hand; index it, flag it (yellow post-it labels are the most convenient), be

comfortable with it; never let your opponent reach a relevant document before you do; the impression of competence and assurance which this creates will stand you in good stead before the court or tribunal before which you appear.

(10) Remember that evidence may be called in civil cases to establish a witness' general reputation for untruthfulness. The witness whose reputation is attacked may be cross-examined on particular incidents which may have gained for him that reputation and subsequent witnesses called to speak about it can only state their general beliefs without reference to separate incidents.

(11) Remember the words of Lord Macmillan who said: 'In the discharge of his office, the advocate has a duty to his client, a duty to his opponent, a duty to the court, a duty to himself, and a duty to the State.' Keith Evans in *Advocacy at the Bar* advises that in jury advocacy 'Beware the broad gesture, the extravagant phrase and think carefully before daring to raise your voice'. Generally, adopt a confident but not overbearing style and try to avoid irritating mannerisms: it can be very instructive to watch yourself prepare on video.

7.4 Witnesses

Witnesses may remain in court in all civil proceedings in England unless the judge orders otherwise, but not in criminal proceedings. In criminal cases, witnesses remain outside the court until their evidence is heard.

It is important to explain to each witness the procedure to be adopted by the court. A witness should be advised to use (when sitting behind you) a pen and paper so that he can inform you of his comments on the other evidence. Stress that he should give you the details as they occur to him, since it may be too late at the next adjournment. However, too many notes passing between client and advocate may create the unfortunate impression of lack of preparedness or a client is over anxious.

There are various ways in which you may seek to put at ease your witnesses; for example:

(a) give the witness an estimate of the earliest time he or she may be called to give evidence;

(b) tell him or her in advance not to speak about the evidence being given;

(c) (in a criminal case) he or she must not leave court unless and until 'released' by the judge, but in most cases this will be a mere formality.

If the witnesses do not understand the import of a question, they should always ask for it to be repeated; they should not guess at the answer. They should at all times keep their temper, however much they resent or dispute the questions being asked or the manner of the asking. They should be advised that the other party's advocate or representative is merely doing his job in asking questions of them. They should understand and not resent his or her behaviour and certainly should not take the matter personally. Finally, the witness should be advised to speak slowly since the judge will make a handwritten note of all the evidence.

7.5   Modes of address

- County court/Crown Court Judges and deputies: Your Honour.
- Court of Appeal Judge: My Lord/My Lady.
- Employment Appeal Tribunal Judge or lay member: Sir/Madam.
- High Court Judge or Deputy sitting as a High Court Judge/Court of Appeal Judge: My Lord/My Lady.
- House of Lords: My Lord.
- Tribunal Chairman or members: Sir/Madam.
- Magistrates' or youth court: Sir/Madam; address the whole bench as 'You sir and your colleagues'.
- Old Bailey Judges and the Recorders of Liverpool and Manchester: My Lord/My Lady.
- Queen's Bench/Chancery Division Master: Master or Sir.
- District Judge: Sir/Madam.

Notes

- Try not to refer to a judge as 'you'.
- Do not use 'Your Lordship' in the vocative form; say 'My Lord, the central point is this' and 'Your Lordship will realise'.
- Refer to a barrister opponent as 'my learned friend' and a solicitor as 'my friend'.
- Avoid asking the judge a direct question.
- Bow to the judge as you enter and leave court.
- When in open court, do not leave court unless told by the judge that you may do so.
- Tell your client before he goes into court what the appropriate form of address for the court is.

7.6 Questioning

7.6.1 Preparation

To begin with, it is useful to adapt to the particular judge or tribunal before whom you are appearing. He, she or they may be slow, quick, prepared to listen and discuss legal principles or determined to cut through the cases as quickly as possible. All these things should become evident within the first 15 minutes. Do not be afraid to ask whether the judge/tribunal has been able to read the papers. Remember that your aim is to convince the court of the justness of your case, and that this process will probably not be assisted or achieved by theatrical displays, heavy handed questioning or attacks on the sensibilities and patience of the court itself.

Apply a logical structure to the asking of your questions. Watch as many advocates as you can and try to observe their strengths and weaknesses.

7.6.2 The witnesses

The witness box, or table, is a place of great stress and anxiety. There will sometimes be questions which are distressing for the witness to answer and matters are made easier for all concerned if questions are posed in a calm and confident manner.

Remember that all witnesses are different and thus are to be treated differently. Some (for example, doctors, policemen) may be very familiar with being examined while others may have never appeared in a court or tribunal before. Adapt your questioning to the particular witness' experience, intelligence and attitude to the court. This is not something which you are likely to be able to prepare for, but something of which you should be aware.

You cannot always expect the witness to say in court exactly what is in the witness statement. In conference or a prior meeting, he or she may be self-assured and, while in the box, may change the story, hedge bets or pile on the ifs and buts. If this happens try not to indicate shock or surprise to the court (for example, by an open mouth). If you are completely 'thrown' by a piece of evidence, ask for a short adjournment to take further instructions. It is important always to expect the unexpected and be prepared for it.

Don't badger, harass or interrupt a witness. Knowing the point when it is clear that a witness is not going to change his mind (and there is no point in his doing so) is something which comes with experience. Do not go on pressing a witness past this point; you will annoy both him and the tribunal. If, however, you cannot get a witness to say what you want or expect him to say, then consider rephrasing the question as it may be that he has misunderstood what you are asking.

7.6.3 Other points

It is not wise to 'over prepare'. Whilst careful preparation (and especially mastery of the case) is important, there is a risk if you have prepared to the extent that all your questions and submissions are made parrot fashion (or you find yourself tied to your notes and end up reading them with your head buried down), that you will be unable to deal with interruptions or questions from your court.

Remember also:

- don't speak too quickly – the court/tribunal will want to take notes;
- don't interrupt opponents – if you have to intervene at all try to make any objections gracefully;
- don't engage in theatrics;
- try not to yawn or slouch;
- listen to all evidence with 'visible' interest;
- be polite;
- be brief;
- engage directly with the court rather than looking down at your notes all the time; and above all
- do not bore the court.

In *Advocacy at the Bar* (see Chapter 13, below), Keith Evans advises:

> Learn the rules as best you can and when you have learnt them be ready to break them. Look for new and better ways of doing the job. Regard it as a craft that has to be learnt but never lose sight of the fact that it is an art as well. Learn your trade. Aim to become a craftsman. Aspire to become an artist.

7.7 Order of speeches and evidence

7.7.1 Civil trials

In a civil trial, the claimant's opening speech comes first, followed by its evidence. The defendant then has an opening speech (only, however, in long cases) followed by the defence evidence, the defendant's closing speech and finally, the claimant's closing speech.

7.7.2 Criminal trials

In a criminal trial, the prosecution opens with a speech, then proceeds with evidence. The defence has an opening speech if they intend to call any witness as to fact, followed by their evidence. In the Crown Court, the prosecution have a closing speech which is made before the defence's speech. The prosecution do not have a closing speech in the magistrates' court (see para 8.4.2). The order in a criminal court proceeds in a case with multiple defendants as follows:

(1) Prosecution evidence-in-chief:

    (a) cross-examination on behalf of the first defendant;

    (b) cross-examination on behalf of the second/third, etc, defendant;

    (c) re-examination.

(2) First defendant's opening.

(3) First defendant's evidence-in-chief:

    (a) cross-examination on behalf of the second defendant;

    (b) cross-examination on behalf of the third, etc, defendant;

    (c) cross-examination on behalf of the prosecution;

    (d) re-examination.

(4) Second defendant's (third, etc) evidence-in-chief, etc.

(5) Prosecution's closing speech.

(6) First defendant's closing speech.

(7) Second defendant's closing speech.

7.7.3 Employment tribunals

In a normal case where dismissal is admitted, the employer opens with a speech followed by their evidence. Then, the employee's evidence and closing speech are given, followed by the employer's closing speech. If, however, it was a discrimination case, the applicant would normally begin since he/she bears the onus of proof.

7.7.4 Opening speeches

Begin by asking the court or tribunal whether they have read any papers. All members of an employment tribunal, for example, will almost certainly have seen the originating application, notice of appearance and any other court documents. Many judges now read the papers before starting the case. Opening speeches are not encouraged. In opening, as in other aspects of the trial, put yourself in the shoes of the judge or tribunal and ask yourself what you would want to hear from the advocate if you were presiding at the particular trial or hearing. In most cases in the High Court, opening skeleton arguments are required (see *Practice Direction: Case Management* [1995] 1 WLR 262), although sometimes it is not possible because of, for example, a late switch. It may be appropriate to then go through the bundle, and you should ensure that it is in logical order well before the trial or hearing. Ask the court whether they would prefer to read the documents for themselves or whether you should read them aloud. The general practice in the Chancery Division sitting in open court is that the documents be read aloud. At this stage, it is also a good idea to list the witnesses you intend to call (and to state why they are being called). Do not, however, go into a lengthy discussion of what you hope the witnesses will say.

As a general rule, do not make an opening speech if only one witness is to give evidence. It may be helpful at this stage to identify in logical order the points the court will have to decide, although it is neither necessary or desirable to give a full legal exposition of them. Citation of cases should await the closing speech but it may be helpful to present an outline chronology and list of characters. Generally, such chronologies presented at the opening of the case should aim to be neutral and, if possible, agreement should be reached with the other side on the contents.

Do not commit yourself too much in opening, or 'open too high' as it is known; if your witnesses do not bear out in their evidence the propositions you contend for in opening, you could be seriously embarrassed and the judge may doubt the genuineness of your case.

There may be issues which by the time of the trial have been agreed by the parties and will no longer be the subject of argument. If this is the case and it is not apparent to the court from the material already before it, then the issues should be identified in opening. It is usual for the opposing advocate formally to state that he agrees that the particular point is no longer in issue.

7.8   Examination-in-chief

7.8.1   Examining witnesses

Remember that your witnesses, unless they have been to court before, will probably be nervous. Use the opportunity of getting them to state their name, address and occupation to put them at their ease. If they are particularly nervous, try and reassure them initially with a few simple and uncontroversial questions to enable them to find their feet. If a witness appears on behalf of a company or firm, their position within that business should be stated. Likewise, expert witnesses should be asked to give their professional qualifications and an indication of the experience and expertise.

7.8.2   Leading the witness

The witness may be expected to read out the witness statement or, more commonly, it will stand as their evidence-in-chief, having been pre-read by the judge, and you will be permitted to ask only necessary supplementary questions. This might include dealing with matters raised for the first time in the witness statement(s) served by the other side, or to elaborate matters which are not clear in your own. Do not seek too much indulgence in respect of supplementaries, since you may by doing so lose the judge's sympathy. It is often tactically useful to ask one or two questions so that the witness is not faced with his first questions from your opponent in cross-examination. Do not ask leading questions (those which suggest a particular answer). For instance, it is better to ask 'When is your birthday?' rather than 'Is your birthday 1 January?'. However, valuable time can be saved by asking leading questions on uncontroversial matters, such as the date of commencement of employment, the nature of the business, and work history (although these may be highly contentious in particular cases). It is best to ask your opponent whether he or she objects to 'leading' on such matters.

In order to avoid the risk of asking leading questions, or not being able to think of a good way of framing a question in court so as to avoid leading the witness, you may want to make a list of the questions you want answered in a non-leading form. It is usually a good idea to include in your list the answer you expect in brackets after the question. In that way, if you do not get what you expect from the witness, you can ask follow up questions until you manage to elicit the information you want. If you have a list of questions, you will also be less likely to repeat yourself. It is important not to be seen to be wasting time by asking unnecessary or repetitive questions.

7.8.3 Form of the evidence

Think carefully about the order in which your witnesses should be called. In most cases, there will be one 'lead' witness (for example, the claimant or defendant himself), and usually it is this witness which should be called first. Indeed, the court may raise their eyebrows if the claimant is not called first for his side. In many cases, it will be appropriate to have the evidence build up in a chronological sequence, sometimes issue by issue, as most courts will be reluctant to break the logical form of the evidence unless there is good reason to do so.

If you are in difficulty because a witness (for example, an expert witness) is only available at a particular time, explain to the court the reasons for this and ask if he may be called out of turn or interposed in the evidence of another.

7.8.4 Other points

Examination according to Richard Du Cann in *The Art of the Advocate*, 1982, Penguin, should be 'a form of spontaneous conversation, between examiner and examined'. To achieve this, the following should be noted:

(1) When you have completed your questioning, make sure that you have got the whole story out; check your statement carefully at the end. Remember that you will not get a second chance.

(2) Do not be afraid to bring out your weak points; it is better that they first come out in evidence-in-chief if they are bound to arise anyway.

(3) Avoid the temptation to comment on a witness' answer.

7.9 Cross-examination

Most people view cross-examination as the most difficult skill of the art of examination. No one (not even the most skilled QC) knows at the start of the cross-examination how he will make out at the end of it, and the witness may be more frightened than you are. Cross-examination is always a risky process. Many people advise never to ask a question you don't know the answer to, but this is probably unrealistic. Remember that the rule against leading questions does not apply in cross-examination. The following principles may help you, but, in the end, it is experience which is invaluable:

(1) Have in mind clear aims in your questioning; your task is to elicit evidence, not to comment as you go along. A great legal point may

in the middle of the cross-examination, but don't
y not have occurred to your opponent and you
to research it well before his closing speech (when
ise possibly hear of it for the first time).

(2) ..e witness is incorrect as to a particular point, but
check that it is material before taking the witness to each and every
error that he may have made in his evidence. It may be easy to show
that a witness is wrong on a particular point, but this is only really
useful if this is a point relevant to your case and you wish to point
to the incorrect evidence in closing your case. It is the evidence
which you are seeking to clarify and prove incorrect where appropriate.
The aim is not to discredit the witness in principle as you will not
enlist the sympathy of the court if you do.

(3) In preparing your cross-examination, look for contradictions both
in the evidence and between the evidence and the documentation,
especially contemporaneous documentation. Imagine how an event
is most likely to have occurred, so that you can put that version to
the witness in order to undermine his version.

(4) Ensure that you do not misquote the witnesses' evidence in asking
questions in cross-examination; you must not mislead the court.

(5) You essentially have a twofold aim in your questioning, to weaken
the case for the other side, and to establish facts favourable to your
own. In doing this, it is commonly said that there are four techniques:
confrontation, undermining, insinuation, and probing. Plan which
one (or combination) you are going to adopt in any series of questions.
One effective method is first to challenge his evidence on peripheral
matters and then to concentrate on the central issue.

(6) Don't feel you have not 'earned your fee' if you don't carry out an
interminable cross-examination – often the shorter the better.
Sometimes you may not need to cross-examine at all.

(7) Keep your questions short; as a general rule, each one should occupy
no more than one line of transcript.

(8) Seek to remain in charge of the cross-examination at all times. Do
not allow the witness to take control. You don't want an opposing
witness to state his case better during cross-examination than in
examination-in-chief.

(9) Ask only one question at a time, and try to ensure that it has a
specific purpose.

(10) Be precise in the questions you ask and don't let the witness score
a point by asking you which question he should answer.

(11) Keep a list of topics to cover and keep a list of outline qu
There are various different approaches to this, but it is unwi
prepare questions in detail before the hearing, since you do n
know precisely what evidence will be given and how it will be given
and it will be all the more difficult to adjust your approach later. You
may wish to keep a list of especially important questions (a 'hit list')
on which you think it likely that you can embarrass the other party's
witnesses; you can return to it when you hit a difficulty in cross-
examination, and you wish to change the subject quickly.

(12) Assess your objectives with each witness. You will probably not need
to discredit every witness for your opponent – sometimes, you may
wish to describe a witness called by your opponent as fair and accurate
in your closing speech. Nothing will be served by a general attack
on his or her credibility.

(13) If you think that a witness is not telling the truth, it is usually better
to try to get him to agree reasons why he might be mistaken (for
example, passage of time, confusion over dates, the circumstances
of an identification, etc). Once you have established these factors,
the witness will probably stick to his original story but it is more
convincing as cross-examination than by merely putting it to the
witness outright that he is wrong. The latter course is likely only to
make the witness more dogmatic as to the strength of his case.

(14) Always be civil to the witness. Do not raise your voice as you don't
want the judge to think 'Thank God he is not cross-examining me'.
Judges (and even more so tribunals) can be especially sensitive to
such unnecessary hostility to a witness. Adopt a gentle inquiring
approach; it may also cause the witness to ease up and relax and be
more willing to agree with your version of events. Do not adopt
Cicero's maxim that 'when you have no basis for argument, abuse
the plaintiff'. You do not want the sympathies of the court or tribunal
to be more with the hunted witness than with you, the hunting
advocate. Remember that you are seeking to discredit the evidence
of the witness rather than the witness himself.

(15) Ensure that you put the whole case to each witness. If, at a later
stage, you will be calling evidence about something material which
the witness in the box said or did, you must put that evidence to
him (you need only put your case to one of your opponent's witnesses).

(16) Do not ask questions of a witness which he does not conceivably
have the knowledge to answer; save matters of expertise for the
expert witness.

(17) Don't expect a witness (and this applies to your own side, too) to help you but don't go off on a fishing trip either. It is often said that if you try to cast about seeing what turns up, you mostly get old boots and bicycle tyres!

(18) Don't ask one question too many – it can be fatal. 'Generally speaking, the weaknesses which the evidence may have and which it is your job to expose are ambiguity, insincerity, faulty perception and erroneous memory.' (Hill and O'Hare, *Civil Litigation*, 1995, p 515.)

7.10 Re-examination

You can only re-examine about matters which arose in cross-examination. Remember that by this stage, your witness may be tired, truculent and just want to get home. Avoid re-examination if the witness has stood up to the rigours of cross-examination unscathed (or virtually so). The court/tribunal will stop an advocate who tries to use re-examination as an opportunity to conduct another examination-in-chief on matters which should have been dealt with the first time around. You also do not want to give the impression to the court or tribunal that you do not like what your witness said in cross-examination and want to pick up the pieces. On the other hand, re-examination has been described as 'a much neglected but sinister art form'. In any case, be short and sharp in re-examination.

7.11 Closing speech

Most courts and tribunals are impatient with long closing speeches, save in highly complex cases. Your aim should be to bring the various strands of fact and law in the case together in such a way that in effect you write the court's decision for them (or the decision which you wish to see promulgated). Take a full note of the judgment. It may be necessary to agree it with the other side in the event of an appeal.

Ensure that the quotations you refer to from the evidence are 100% accurate. In complex cases, it may be appropriate to use written observations or a skeleton argument (the comments of Lightman J on such skeletons in his lecture to the Chancery Bar Association given on 3 June 1998 are very well worth reading). On skeleton arguments in the Court of Appeal, see *Practice Direction (Court of Appeal: Skeleton Arguments and Case Management)* (1997) *The Times,* 7 November. The only disadvantage is that in many cases important ideas may arise from interchanges between you and the court, and the weight given to these may be lessened if they are absent from the written brief you submit. In any event, go through the evidence in a logical order.

Face the difficulties you have fairly and squarely and examine them individually. Remember that a civil court is reluctant, if it can be avoided, to reject the evidence of a witness completely, so approach such an attempt to discredit with caution.

Pick a logical structure for the closing speech organised through a series of submissions. Only cite cases if it is necessary to do so; there is House of Lords authority that you should not do so (*Lambert v Lewis* [1981] 1 All ER 1185). Most judges are very familiar with the leading cases and nothing will be gained by a detailed recitation of the facts of cases unless they are directly in point. Set out simply and clearly the propositions for which you contend; it is only if the court looks puzzled or disapproving that you will need to read the case. Many advocates prefer to prepare the speech in note form only. Others will write out the entire speech word by word. Do what is most comfortable for your style of advocacy. Whichever you prefer, make sure the print you are reading from is sufficiently big so that you are not screwing up your eyes to read it. Try to engage directly with the judge or tribunal rather than merely read a speech.

It is often convenient to prepare copies of the relevant authorities for the court, and place them in a paginated folder. Much time is wasted by the court usher locating and handing up copies of the law reports (even if you have given a full list in beforehand). The court can also mark the copies you submit. Refer back to the comments made by the judge during the hearing, both supportive and hostile to your case.

7.12 After judgment

When judgment has been given, remember to:

- ask for costs if successful (see Chapter 11);
- seek entry of final judgment with a clearly defined order;
- calculate any interest to be awarded (in the High Court interest is payable after judgment under the Judgments Act 1838 unless the judgment provides for payment at a higher contractual rate);
- ask for a stay of execution pending appeal if this is appropriate; and seek payment out of any sums paid into court, if this is appropriate.

8 The Magistrates' Court

The young practitioner, in the first months of practice, is likely to deal with a wide range of matters in the magistrates' court and other courts, including such actions as possession orders and winding up petitions. The vast majority of all crime is dealt with in the magistrates' court. Due to the large number of courts and the fact that it is usually a lay tribunal, the organisation of the courts and the standard of the bench vary enormously. For the novice advocate, his greatest ally in the court will be the clerk, well versed in practice and procedure and in most cases willing to offer advice and assistance. Fellow lawyers are another source of helpful advice: never be afraid to ask them for assistance. Law and procedure in the magistrates' court is covered in the three volume work *Stones Justices' Manual*, Butterworths. There is a new edition published every year and it covers all statutory material relating to the workings of the court and the law for the substantive offences with which the court is concerned. However, most young practitioners carry the one volume work *Blackstone's Criminal Practice*, Blackstone, updated yearly, which covers all the criminal material needed for magistrates' court work.

When you arrive at court to defend, always go and see the Crown Prosecution Service representative first. Find out what their views are about what will happen that day; whether they are opposing bail; whether they have any papers to serve on you; whether they have reviewed the file and will be altering the charges; whether they are in a position to proceed to committal. As soon as you meet your client, he will want to know the answer to these questions.

Next check the legal aid position; whether an application has been made; whether the court are waiting for your client to provide them with more information; then if your client needs to forward proof of benefit or wage slips, then you can ask him to do so.

Once you have this information, you can have a constructive conference with your client.

8.1 Bail

8.1.1 Client in custody

You will often arrive at the magistrates' court to discover that your client has been arrested and been held in the cells overnight. Always take the time and the trouble to explain to your client who you are and what the nature of the hearing is. The prosecution may seek a remand in custody. If so, it will be your responsibility to consider whether to apply for bail. Your client may have been remanded in custody by the police after charge on the basis that there are grounds for denying bail. If your client is produced in custody, then you must take instructions about whether he wants a bail application. (Applying for bail is often a greater preoccupation for your client at his first appearance than the offence itself or what will happen to him at the end of this case.)

Sometimes, it may be sensible to advise your client that a bail application at that stage would not be in his best interests, for example, if he has not found a suitable address, but could do so within a week or so, or if a potential surety has not been contacted yet.

8.1.2 Bail Act 1976

Bail is governed by the Bail Act 1976 (see, generally, *Blackstone's Criminal Practice*, para D5.1 *et seq*). Section 4 creates a presumption in favour of bail, subject to Sched 1 which lays down certain circumstances in which the grant of bail may legitimately be refused. These include:

(1) If the court is satisfied that there are substantial grounds for believing that the defendant, if released, would:

   (a) fail to surrender to custody; or

   (b) commit an offence while on bail; or

   (c) interfere with witnesses or otherwise obstruct the course of justice.

(2) If the defendant should be kept in custody for his own protection.

(3) If, owing to lack of time since proceedings were commenced, it has not been practicable to obtain sufficient information to make a decision as regards bail.

The Crown Court also has jurisdiction to grant bail where a person has been committed to it, is appealing against a decision of the magistrates' court or is appealing to the Divisional Court by way of case stated. There is also power for the Crown Court to grant bail during a trial on indictment. An application may be made to the High Court for bail if the magistrates' court refuses to grant bail or if the defendant is applying to have the decision of the magistrates' court or Crown Court quashed.

8.1.3 Bail proceedings

The prosecution opens the argument by outlining the objections to bail. The defence advocate then replies. Consider each of the points that the prosecution makes. Do they stand up to close analysis? Does any real evidence support them? If necessary, attack any assumptions on which the prosecution bases the allegations through cross-examination. In your submissions, consider the following factors:

- the nature and seriousness of the offence and the possible method of dealing with it. If the offence is not serious or a custodial sentence is unlikely at trial, then it is more likely that bail will be granted;
- your client's character, antecedents, associations and community ties. Would he have a lot to lose by failing to surrender?;
- your client's previous bail record. Has he previously failed to answer bail or committed offences whilst on bail? If he has not, this is some indication that he will not abuse the grant of bail. If he has, be ready with an explanation for the past lapse(s) and why the court ought to disregard them when considering bail on this occasion;
- the strength of the prosecution's case.

Make your submissions in a crisp and attractive manner. Remember that the court has probably heard the same submissions hundreds of times before.

8.1.4 Conditions of bail

Bail may be either granted unconditionally or subject to conditions. It is sensible for a defendant whose position is on the line to offer conditions to the court. Conditions frequently imposed include:

- to reside at a specified address;
- to report to a local police station on a daily or weekly basis;
- to obey a curfew;

- not to enter a certain area or building or go within a specified distance of a certain address;
- not to contact prosecution witnesses;
- to surrender his passport.

Other conditions may be attached depending on the nature of the offence. Try to think of conditions that will allay the magistrates' concerns. In addition, one or more sureties may be offered. A surety will render himself liable to forfeit a specified sum of money should the defendant fail to answer to his bail. If your client has sureties, make sure that you explain clearly the significance of the obligation and the consequences if the defendant absconds.

If bail is granted, the date of the next court appearance will be fixed and it will be an offence for the defendant to fail to answer to his bail at that date and time. If bail is refused, the defendant will be remanded in custody (for the period of remand, see para 8.1.6, below). An appeal against the refusal of bail lies to the Crown Court. The hearing of the application is normally in chambers.

8.1.5 Applications for bail

A defendant may only make two bail applications as of right. The first is immediately upon being brought to court and the second following a period of remand in custody. Should that second argued application fail, the defendant may not in general present argument on the subsequent occasions when he appears before the court, although each time the court should nominally consider whether he ought to remain in custody. The above is a summary of the position by virtue of Pt IIA of Sched 1 to the Bail Act 1976, which was intended to give statutory effect to the decision in *R v Nottingham Justices ex p Davies* [1981] QB 38.

From the third remand hearing, the bench can refuse to hear an argued bail application unless there has been a change in circumstances since the last such application. Examples of a change in circumstances include an offer of a surety, the availability of an offer of employment or a place of residence, or some new evidence coming to light about the charges.

The conditions of bail may be varied, for example, if it is not possible for a defendant to comply with a condition to report to the police station on a particular occasion. Either the prosecution or the defence may make an application. At the application (which is usually to the magistrates' court which granted the bail, but may be to the Crown Court to which the defendant was committed), the reasons for the request to vary the conditions are stated. It is better to try to reach an agreement with the prosecution beforehand if possible.

8.1.6 Remand in custody

A case may be adjourned and a defendant granted bail for as long as the court deems necessary (see ss 5 and 10 of the Magistrates' Courts Act 1980 (MCA 1980)). Strict rules regulate the period during which a defendant may be remanded in custody. Unless a defendant consents to being remanded in his absence, the period of remand must not exceed eight clear days (s 128(6) of the MCA 1980). Where he consents and certain conditions are satisfied, a defendant may be remanded in his absence on his second or subsequent remand for up to 28 days (s 128A of the MCA 1980). If a defendant is already detained under a custodial sentence, he may be remanded in custody for up to 28 days or until his anticipated release date, whichever is the shorter period (s 131 of the MCA 1980).

8.1.7 Appealing against a bail decision – the defence

If you apply for bail and are refused, then you should ask for a certificate of full argument in order to appeal. If you are instructed to appeal the decision, you can apply to either the Crown Court or the High Court, or both, where the matter will be heard again.

8.1.8 Appealing against a bail decision – the prosecution

The prosecution has a right to appeal against the grant of bail in the magistrates' court (s 1 of the Bail (Amendment) Act 1993).

This is applicable in cases where the defendant is charged with an offence which carries a sentence of at least five years' imprisonment, or is taking a vehicle without consent, or aggravated vehicle taking.

In order to appeal, the prosecution must have objected to bail when the application was made (s 1(3)(a)), and must give oral notice of the appeal (s 1(3)(b)) when bail is granted and serve written notice of the appeal on the magistrates' court and the defendant within two hours of the hearing at which bail was granted (s 1(4)). (This procedure is inserted into the Bail Act at s 93(A)). If the prosecution decides to appeal against a grant of bail, then the defendant will remain in custody until the appeal is heard. The appeal must be heard within 48 hours, excluding weekends and public holidays (s 1(8)). The appeal is heard by a judge in the Crown Court.

8.2   Initial proceedings

8.2.1 Advance information

In deciding how to proceed with the case, it is of great assistance to know the case against your client. If the offence is triable either way, the defence is entitled to advance information of either the written statements upon which the prosecution propose to rely at trial, or a summary of the case against him (the Magistrates' Court (Advance Information) Rules 1985; see *Blackstone's Criminal Practice*, para D4.12). You may find that some prosecutors are prepared to supply the information in respect of summary only offences. A defendant is entitled to refuse to take any step in the proceedings until advanced disclosure of the prosecution case has been forthcoming. A defendant may, however, waive his right to this information.

8.2.2 Mode of trial

Except in the case of summary only offences, the mode of trial must be determined by the magistrates' court. Under the new 'plea before venue' procedure, before determining the mode of trial, the court will invite the defendant to indicate his plea, having explained to him that he may be committed to the Crown Court for sentence if the court considers that its powers of sentence are insufficient (s 49 of the Criminal Procedure and Investigations Act 1996 (CPIA 1996)(amending s 17 of the MCA 1980)). If the defendant indicates a plea of guilty, he will be treated as convicted. The court will then proceed itself to sentence or committal to the Crown Court for sentence.

Once you have considered the advance information in the case, you can inform the court that you are ready to deal with 'plea before venue'. The clerk of the court will then read out the charge or charges which are the subject of the either way offence to the defendant and explain to him the procedure before asking him how he wishes to plead.

If the defendant indicates that he will plead guilty, then the prosecutor opens the facts of the offence, and any previous convictions, to the court, and then the court hears mitigation from the defence. If it is reasonable to expect that the magistrates' court has sufficient sentencing powers to deal with your client, then you should persuade the magistrates to accept jurisdiction and present the mitigation. The magistrates will then decide whether they have sufficient powers to sentence.

If the magistrates decide that they have sufficient powers they will say so and either sentence then or adjourn for reports. If they decide that they do not then they will commit the defendant to the Crown Court for sentence by a Crown Court judge and two lay magistrates.

Sentencing powers in the magistrates' court are limited to a maximum sentence of six months' imprisonment for one offence triable either way, or 12 months' imprisonment for two or more triable either way offences. This applies no matter how many summary only offences the defendant is charged with at the same time.

If the defendant fails to indicate a plea or indicates a plea of not guilty, the court will hear representations (if any) as to the appropriate forum from the prosecution and the defence. At this stage, the court is only concerned with the gravity of the offence. The defendant's previous convictions are irrelevant and should not be brought to the attention of the court. If the magistrates feel able to deal with the case, the defendant is given a choice of which court he wishes to try the offence. He must be warned that if he elects summary trial he may still be committed to the Crown Court for sentence if the court considers its powers of punishment are insufficient or a longer sentence is necessary for the protection of the public. In respect of offences triable either way, if your client does not wish to be tried in the magistrates' court, he cannot be compelled to be so tried.

8.3 Committal for trial

If the defendant elects trial on indictment or if the magistrates decline jurisdiction, the defendant will have to be committed to the Crown Court for trial. This will take one of two forms and a decision has to be made about which is the more appropriate. The Criminal Procedure and Investigations Act 1996 now governs the procedure at committal for all offences where the investigation began on or before 1 April 1997. Committal bundles will be sent to you by post or handed to you at court by the Crown Prosecution Service. After looking at the statements, you will have to ask yourself whether there is a *prima facie* case that your client is guilty of an indictable offence. The test is whether a reasonable jury properly directed could convict on the prosecution evidence. Committal may be by way of a 'new style' or 'paper' committal under s 6(2) of the MCA 1980 whereby all parties agree to committal to the appropriate Crown Court. Alternatively, an 'old style' committal, with consideration of evidence under s 6(1) of the MCA 1980, may be appropriate where the defence believes that there is a realistic chance of a submission of no case succeeding (see, generally, *Blackstone's Criminal Practice*, para D7.9 *et seq*).

8.3.1 Section 6(2) committal

In a s 6(2) committal, the court does not even read or have read to it the written evidence tendered. The documents are simply handed up by the prosecution. The clerk will usually ask the defence counsel or solicitor whether he agrees to a s 6(2) committal. If he agrees, the matter will be committed to the Crown Court without further consideration.

If the defence accepts that this test is passed, then the prosecution must supply to the court the originals of the statements in the case and the case will be formally committed to the Crown Court.

In accordance with the Criminal Procedure and Investigations Act 1996, the defendant will be told that he must give orders in writing to the prosecution, within 14 days of that date, of any witnesses whom he wishes to give live evidence at his trial.

8.3.2 Committal with consideration of evidence

The CPIA 1996 has effected a change to s 6(1) committals. At the old s 6(1) committals, the prosecution was entitled to call live witnesses to give evidence. The defence might also call evidence if it wishes to. There remain a few cases (where the investigation began before 1 April 1997) where this form of s 6(1) committal is still available. These are becoming more rare.

Because the days of such committals are not long gone, clients who have successfully contested cases in this way in the past may demand them of you now. They must be advised that the law has changed and that the circumstances in which a s 6(1) committal will be held are now very much narrowed for all offences where the investigation began on or after 1 April 1997.

In a new s 6(1) committal, the prosecution will outline the case and explain any relevant points of law, before tendering the written evidence. This may be read through or, with the leave of the court, summarised. No witnesses are called. No evidence is tendered by the defence. The defence may then make a submission of no case to answer. A submission may be made for example where as a matter of law the statements do not reveal a *prima facie* case to answer, or there is a clear defence (for example, self-defence) or the defence allege mistaken identity. The prosecution has a right to reply to the submission, after which the magistrates will decide whether or not to commit.

8.3.3 Notes on committal

For alleged offences in which the criminal investigation began on or after 1 April 1997, the statutory rules set out in the CPIA 1996 now apply (see *Blackstone's Criminal Practice*, para D7.17). A witness statement tendered at committal may without further proof be read as evidence at the trial of the accused unless the defendant objects (see paras 1(2) and 1(3)(c) of Sched 2 to the CPIA 1996). The objection must be made in writing to the Crown Court and the prosecution within 14 days of committal (r 8 of the Magistrates' Courts Rules 1981). Notwithstanding any objection, the court may order that the objection shall have no effect if the court considers that, in the interests of justice, the evidence should be read (para 1(4) of the CPIA 1996).

You should remember to ask for bail afresh at committal proceedings. If your client is legally aided, you should ask for his legal aid to be extended to the Crown Court.

8.3.4 The defence statement

The duty to give notice of alibi under s 11 of the Criminal Justice Act 1967 has been repealed and replaced by the wider duty to provide a defence statement under s 5 of the CPIA 1996. The defence statement sets out in general terms the nature of the defence, the matters on which the defendant takes issue with the prosecution (with reasons), and the details of his alibi (if any). This should be served within 14 days of primary disclosure by the prosecution. In the Crown Court, the defendant must make a defence statement. If he fails to do so, secondary disclosure by the prosecution (of material which may reasonably be expected to assist the defence advanced in the defence statement) will not be triggered. Furthermore, the court or jury may draw inferences from the defendant's failure to disclose properly his defence or if he puts forward an inconsistent defence at trial (see s 11 of the CPIA 1996).

A defence statement is voluntary for matters dealt with in the magistrates' court (or Youth court). If one is served, it triggers secondary disclosure, and the court may allow comment or inferences to be drawn from the late or inconsistent disclosure as above (for disclosure generally, see *Blackstone's Criminal Practice*, para D6.1 *et seq*).

Remember that in certain circumstances, the court will be permitted to draw adverse inferences from silence under ss 34–37 of the Criminal Justice and Public Order Act 1994 (see *Blackstone's Criminal Practice*, para F19.4 *et seq*).

8.3.5 Summary trial

Before a summary trial, the prosecution may serve upon the defence written statements pursuant to s 9 of the Criminal Justice Act 1969. These will be tendered in evidence in their written form unless the defence serves a notice requiring the maker to be called to give oral testimony. The notice should be served within seven days and it is important that such a deadline is not missed. In trials of summary only offences, the defence is not entitled to advance information (see para 8.2.1 above) and accordingly the first indication you may have as to the nature of the case against the defendant will be when the witnesses give their testimony at trial. Never be afraid to ask for sight of the statements; the Crown can only say no. Often, a letter to the prosecution after the defendant has entered his not guilty plea requesting a 'courtesy bundle' will bear fruit. However, you should not be afraid to request an adjournment to take instructions on matters raised.

8.4   Prosecuting in the magistrates' court

8.4.1 Crown Prosecution Service

As presently constituted, the Crown Prosecution Service (CPS) is insufficiently staffed to conduct prosecutions in all its courts using its own personnel. Accordingly, recourse is frequently made to solicitors and junior barristers who act as agents. The work performed by CPS agents falls into two types: the remand lists on which 20–30 cases appear and trials which concern one case alone. The latter requires preparation on the law and a sound understanding of the facts. The former is more demanding because of the volume of work involved. Any number of matters may arise regarding bail, adjournments, custody time limits etc, and a volume on criminal procedure ought to be kept readily at hand.

8.4.2 Speeches

It should be remembered that in the magistrates' court (unlike the Crown Court) the prosecution has no right to make a closing speech. Accordingly, the opening speech must be used to best advantage and a pre-emptive strike made in respect of any significant argument which may be raised by the defence. For example, if you are prosecuting in respect of a pub fight and the prosecution witnesses are likely to appear as violent as the defendant, it is worth making a point in opening which may defuse the attack ultimately made upon them. You should take the opportunity to state that whatever view one takes of the victims, it does not excuse the act alleged.

There is one occasion where the prosecution does have a right to reply. Where the defence makes representations as to the law, it is open to the prosecution to correct any misleading or inaccurate remarks made. It is therefore imperative that the prosecutor is aware of the elements of the offence alleged and what may or may not amount to a defence.

8.5 Sentencing

8.5.1 Custody

The minimum age for a sentence of imprisonment is 21 (see s 1(1) of the Criminal Justice Act 1982). The maximum length of a prison sentence is prescribed by the statute creating the offence. It should be noted, however, that the longest custodial sentence which may be imposed by a magistrates' court is six months for an individual offence or 12 months in total for two or more triable either way offences (see ss 31 and 133 of the MCA 1980). A court may not pass a sentence of imprisonment on an offender unless it is satisfied:

- that the offence or the combination of the offence and one or more offences associated with it, was so serious that only custody can be justified; or
- where the offence is a violent or sexual offence, that only custody would be adequate to protect the public from serious harm (see s 1(2) of the Criminal Justice Act 1991 (CJA 1991)).

Any custodial sentence passed must be commensurate with the seriousness of the offence(s) (see s 2(2)(a) of the CJA 1991). It should be noted that the new Crime (Sentences) Act 1997 requires the Crown Court to impose an automatic life sentence for the second of certain 'serious offences' (see *Blackstone's Criminal Practice*, para E1.22).

The custodial sentences available for offenders under 21 are detention in a young offender institution, detention under s 53 of the Children and Young Persons Act 1933 (CYPA 1933), custody for life, detention at Her Majesty's pleasure and (when the relevant provisions come into force) a secure training order (see *Blackstone's Criminal Practice*, para E3.1 *et seq*). Lengths of sentence depend upon the age of the offender, with a minimum being 21 days and the maximum that which would be imposed in respect of an adult offender. For the most serious of offences, prolonged periods of detention may be imposed by virtue of s 53(2) of the CYPA 1933. Offenders suffering from a mental disorder may be detained in a secure unit by virtue of a hospital order made pursuant to ss 37–43 of the Mental Health Act 1983.

8.5.2 Suspended sentences

Sections 22–27 of the Powers of the Criminal Courts Act 1973 (PCCA 1973) permit courts in certain *exceptional* circumstances to pass suspended sentences. In brief, the requirements are as follows:

* the offender is over 21;

* the term of imprisonment does not exceed two years;

* the operational period, that is, the time during which the threat of activation hangs over the offender, is between 12 months and two years;

* it would be otherwise appropriate for a custodial sentence to be passed; and

* a suspended sentence can be justified by the exceptional circumstances of the case.

An offence committed during the operational period will activate the sentence which has been suspended unless there are good grounds for not doing so. If no further offences are committed during this period, the period of custody remains unserved. It is possible to combine a suspended sentence with a suspended sentence supervision order (s 26 of the PCCA 1973). This has the effect of providing the support normally obtained under a probation order, for the duration of the operational period. A suspended sentence can also be combined with a community service order, curfew order or fine.

8.5.3 Community sentences

The Criminal Justice Act 1991 introduced the concept of the 'community sentence'. This may include a probation order, a community service order, a combination order, a curfew order, a supervision order or an attendance centre order. A court may not impose a community sentence unless:

- it is satisfied that the offence was serious enough to warrant such a sentence;
- the particular order(s) are the most suitable for the offender;
- the restrictions on liberty are commensurate to the seriousness of the offence(s) (and previous convictions and failures to respond to court orders in the past may be taken into account).

Before forming an opinion as to the suitability of an offender for most community sentences, the court must obtain and consider a pre-sentence report (s 7(3) of the CJA 1991, see *Blackstone's Criminal Practice*, para E4.1). Breach of a community sentence will render an offender liable to a fine, a further community sentence and/or resentencing for the original offence (see *Blackstone's Criminal Practice*, para E4.6 *et seq*).

Community service

The power to impose this penalty is contained in ss 14–17 of the PCCA 1973. The following conditions apply:
- the offender must be 16 or over;
- he must have been convicted of an imprisonable offence;
- a pre-sentence report must be obtained;
- for offences committed prior to 1 October 1997 the offender must consent (this is no longer the case for offences committed on or after that date under amendments to the PCCA 1973 by the Crime (Sentences) Act 1997);
- the number of hours to be worked is between 40 and 240 (usually completed within 12 months).

Probation

The court derives its power to place an offender on probation from ss 2–3 of the PCCA 1973. The following conditions apply:
- the offender must be 16 or over;
- the court must be satisfied that the supervision of the offender by a probation officer is desirable to secure his rehabilitation, protect the public from harm or prevent the commission of further offences by him;
- the period of probation must be between six months and three years;
- for offences committed prior to 1 October 1997, the offender must consent (see above);

- additional requirements may be attached to the order, for example, residence at a specified location, treatment at a hospital, as an out-patient and/or at a day centre for mental condition, drug or alcohol dependency (consent is required for these);
- a pre-sentence report must be obtained if additional requirements are to be attached.

Combination orders

An order may be made combining probation and community service in the form of a combination order by virtue of s 11 of the CJA 1991. The following conditions apply:

- the offender must be 16 or over;
- a pre-sentence report must be obtained;
- the court must be satisfied that the making of a combination order is desirable to secure the offender's rehabilitation, protect the public from harm or prevent the commission of further offences by him;
- the period of supervision must be between one and three years and the number of hours of community service between 40 and 100;
- additional requirements may be attached to the probation part of the order;
- consent is required for offences committed before 1 October 1997 and where additional requirements are to be imposed (see above).

Curfew orders

The court may impose a curfew order requiring the offender to remain at a specified place during specified periods by virtue of s 12 of the CJA 1991. The following conditions apply:

- the offender must be 10 or over;
- the curfew must be for between two and 12 hours in any one day;
- for offenders under 16, periods of curfew cannot be imposed beyond three months from the date of the order, for those over 16, the maximum period is six months;
- consent is required for offences committed before 1 October 1997 (see above);
- the court must obtain and consider information about the place proposed to be specified in the order and as to the attitude of persons likely to be affected by his presence there;

- if the offender is under 16, the court must obtain and consider information about his family circumstances and the likely effect of such an order on those circumstances;

- where arrangements are available, a curfew order may require the electronic monitoring of the offender's whereabouts during the curfew periods.

8.5.4 Other sentences

Fine

The Crown Court may impose any level of fine (s 32(1) of the Criminal Law Act 1977). The magistrates' court, however, is limited to certain 'scales' which are set out in the statute creating the offence. The up to date scales are summarised on the inside cover of *Stones Justices' Manual*. Fines are imposed according to levels between 1 and 5. The current level 1 is a fine not exceeding £200 and level 5 is a fine not exceeding £5,000. The court may order a period of imprisonment in default of a payment of a fine.

Absolute or conditional discharge

Where a defendant is convicted of an offence and the court is of the opinion that it is inexpedient to inflict punishment, it may make an order discharging him absolutely or subject to the condition that he commits no offence during a specified period not exceeding three years.

Deferment

The court may defer sentence for up to six months if it is satisfied that it is in the interests of justice to do so (s 1 of the PCCA 1973). This may be appropriate where some event in the near future is expected to influence the court's decision on sentence, for example, employment, treatment for drug or alcohol addiction.

Bind over

The court may bind over a person to keep the peace or to be of good behaviour in a specified sum. The period of the order and the amount of the recognisance entered are in the discretion of the court. Refusal to enter into a recognisance may result in imprisonment. A person who does not comply with the bind over may forfeit some or all of the recognisance.

Road traffic offences

The minutiae of endorsement and disqualification are dealt with comprehensively in *Wilkinson's Road Traffic Offences*, 1997: Sweet & Maxwell, *Blackstone's Criminal Practice* or *Stones Justices' Manual*.

Other orders

Courts also have the power to order confiscation, deportation, exclusion orders, forfeiture, restitution orders, restriction orders, destruction and compensation in money terms for damage caused or personal injury sustained.

8.6   The youth court

8.6.1 Procedure

The youth court is a part of the magistrates' court. The atmosphere is less formal, the press and public are not admitted and the form of oath and the mode of address of the parties differ from that in the adult court. The juvenile is referred to by his forename, although the member of the bench is still addressed as Sir or Madam. There is a 'finding of guilt' and 'order made upon finding of guilt' rather than a 'conviction' and 'sentence'.

8.6.2 Jurisdiction

The youth court has jurisdiction in respect of all those who have not yet reached 18. Persons under that age may still be tried on indictment or be tried in the magistrates' court in appropriate circumstances. If a juvenile is charged alone or with others who are also juveniles, his first appearance will be in the youth court. If charged jointly with an adult or adults, the juvenile will appear with them in the magistrates' court. The juvenile has no right to be tried on indictment. Under s 24 of the MCA 1980, there are three situations in which a juvenile either must be tried in the Crown Court or the magistrates have a discretion whether to deal with him themselves or commit him for trial:

* a juvenile charged with homicide must be tried on indictment;

- if a juvenile is charged jointly with an adult, the magistrates have a discretion to commit them both to trial if the court considers it necessary in the interests of justice;

- if the offence is punishable by 14 years or more imprisonment and the juvenile is at least 10 and not more than 17, he must be committed for trial if the magistrates consider that in the event of him being found guilty, he should be detained for a long period under s 53(2) of the CYPA 1933. If they are not of that opinion, he must be tried summarily.

If the juvenile is to be tried summarily, he will be tried in the youth court unless jointly charged with an adult or the offence with which he is charged arises out of circumstances connected with which an adult is charged, in which case there is a discretion to try the juvenile in the adult magistrates' court. Reference should be made to *Blackstone's Criminal Practice* for a more detailed consideration.

8.6.3 Sentencing

There are complex and detailed provisions in respect of the sentencing of juveniles, again reference should be made to *Blackstone's Criminal Practice*. The Children and Young Persons Acts 1933 and 1969, Powers of the Criminal Courts 1973, Criminal Justice Acts 1982 and 1991 and Magistrates' Courts Act 1980 all deal with the maximum levels of punishment and range of measures available. Broadly, there are three courts that have power to sentence a juvenile. These are the youth court, the magistrates' court and the Crown Court. The range of sentences available include detention in a young offender institution, a supervision order, an attendance centre order, a fine, compensation, and the court may also bind over the parent or guardian of an offender under 16. The powers of the courts are different and depend upon the age of the offender.

The Crown Court

All the sentences provided by statute in respect of juveniles are available to the Crown Court following a conviction of the juvenile on indictment. By s 56(1) of the CYPA 1933, the Crown Court should remit the case for sentence to the youth court after conviction (except in cases of homicide), unless satisfied that it would be undesirable to do so. In reality, the majority of juveniles convicted in the Crown Court are also sentenced there. The Crown Court has more limited powers following a committal for sentence from the youth court under s 37 of the MCA

1980. Then, the maximum sentence in a young offender institution that may be imposed on a juvenile aged 15, 16 or 17 is 24 months.

The youth court

Where the youth court has made a finding of guilt (or where the case has been remitted to it), the maximum sentence in a young offender institution that may be imposed on a juvenile aged 15, 16 or 17, is six months or where two or more indictable offences are dealt with 12 months. The youth court can commit a juvenile aged 15, 16 or 17 to the Crown Court for sentence, if the seriousness of the offence merits a greater sentence than it can impose.

The magistrates' court

The sentencing powers of the magistrates' court in relation to juveniles are limited to an absolute or conditional discharge, a fine, compensation, endorsement, disqualification and costs. If the magistrates consider that some other sentence is appropriate, the juvenile must be remitted to the youth court for sentence.

8.7   The plea in mitigation

The first taste of advocacy for many solicitors and barristers will be the plea in mitigation. This is one of the most difficult speeches to make because the bench or judge will probably have heard it all before. If the defendant pleads guilty, then the prosecution will briefly outline the facts and circumstances of the case before the defendant is entitled to a speech in mitigation. If the defendant is found guilty, then there is also an opportunity to make a speech in mitigation before sentence is passed.

In mitigation, the defendant's representative should always try to state the circumstances of the case as realistically as possible. In many cases, there is simply no point in trying to convince the tribunal that your client is free of all blame and has a spotless character. Submissions in mitigation which amount to denials of elements of the offence are inappropriate since the defendant has already pleaded guilty or been found to be guilty. Try to get instructions on anything which might explain the defendant's conduct or any special considerations which affect him. If he has given evidence, make sure your submissions accord with what he said in evidence.

It is possible to call the defendant to give evidence in support of his mitigation but this is rarely done. There is a risk that the defendant may make matters worse for himself. The judge or magistrate will normally make a decision in his own mind as to whether the offence merits either a tariff sentence (that is, the judge is making an example of your client's wrongdoing showing that society will not tolerate such conduct and that by punishing him he is intending it to have a deterrent effect) or a sentence which is specifically designed to rehabilitate the particular defendant. It is normally appropriate that you bring to the attention of the court:

- the previous good character of the offender (if applicable);

- if he has previous convictions, try and distinguish them from what he is charged with today. Did he plead guilty on the last occasion? How serious is this offence in relation to his previous offences? Did he play a minor role in the offence?;

- his family background. Does he come from a stable background? Is he married with children? Does he have a job? How long has he had the job? Is he in full time education/apprenticeship?;

- his place of abode: fixed or living in a cardboard box under Waterloo Bridge? How long has he been living there?;

- has he shown any remorse for what he has done? Is he willing to make restitution?;

- did he make a statement under caution? This is particularly important when you are dealing with a persistent offender who has pleaded not guilty on previous occasions and has been found guilty, who here admits the crime and saves the police the inconvenience and expense of investigating the crime;

- has he co-operated with the police? Did he acquiesce during the arrest and assist the police in tracing others who may have been involved in the crime?;

- it is always important to stress to the court the reasons why he may have committed the offence (for example, stealing food from a supermarket when he has no money to pay for food, committing an assault after being provoked or any other extenuating circumstances);

- the age of the offender. If dealing with a juvenile, the magistrates' court will normally pass a sentence to enable the juvenile to reform. When dealing with someone in their 60s, sentence again may be shorter than the norm;

- guilty plea. An offender who pleads guilty can normally expect a reduction of between 25 and 33% in sentence. This is particularly so in rape or sexual assault cases where the victim is spared the obvious discomfort and humiliation of giving evidence.

You may seek to persuade the court that the defendant was acting completely out of character. If so, it may help to have a character reference or call witnesses to give evidence to this effect (for example, the defendant's employer or somebody of standing who has known him for some time). Try to steer the judge towards a particular type of sentence, which you believe will not only punish the offender but also enable him to be rehabilitated. It may be that your client is particularly suitable for a community service order. Explain the restrictions that such an order would have on the defendant's free time. If the defendant has any particular skills (for example, gardening, painting and decorating, patience with old people), make sure that you emphasise this fact to the judge. Request an adjournment so that a pre-sentence report can be obtained to indicate suitability for a community sentence. Most importantly, be realistic.

Be careful not to make matters worse for your client. Do not suggest a fine if the defendant has no hope of paying it. Be brief and concise. Only stress matters particular to your client.

8.8   Applying for legal aid

The relevant provisions and procedure are contained in the Legal Aid Act 1988, Pt III of the General Regulations (see, generally, *Blackstone's Criminal Practice*, para D27.1 *et seq*). An application to a magistrates' court for legal aid should be made in writing (to a justices' clerk). The prescribed form must be obtained from the court office. The form requires details of the nature of the proceedings, the reason why legal aid is necessary and details of the solicitor that the applicant wishes to act for him. A statement of the applicant's means is usually also required. The grant of legal aid may be subject to a contribution order depending on the applicant's resources. At most magistrates' courts, the application is dealt with administratively by the solicitor or counsel lodging both forms at the court prior to or on the day of the hearing. Where it has not been possible to lodge the forms until the day, you should ask the court to indicate informally whether the case is suitable for legal aid (that is, that it would be in the interests of justice for legal aid to be granted).

Most applications are made to the magistrates' court. If such an application is refused, the applicant may make a further application to the Crown Court which has concurrent jurisdiction to grant legal aid for proceedings before itself. It is not possible to apply to the Crown Court for legal aid for committal proceedings or for summary trial. It may be possible to apply to the Area Committee for review of the decision. This is available where the applicant has been charged with an indictable offence, and the application was refused as not being in the interests of justice, not because of the applicant's means. Notification of intention to apply to the committee must be given within 14 days of the refusal of the initial application. Further, the application for legal aid must have been made at least 21 days before the date (if any) fixed for the hearing. Without prejudice to this, the applicant may renew his application either orally to the court or to the justices' clerk. On the second application, a clerk must grant legal aid or refer the application to the court. It is then in the court's discretion whether legal aid is granted. Appeal against the court's decision to refuse legal aid is then by way of judicial review in the Divisional Court.

9 Possession Orders and Winding Up Petitions

9.1 Possession orders

We consider these applications because they are often conducted by new entrants to the legal profession.

9.1.1 Scope

It is unlawful to obtain possession of residential premises without a court order for possession (Protection from Eviction Act 1977). A distinction is drawn between business tenancies and those in respect of dwelling houses. The grounds on which a person may be entitled to possession are set out in the Rent Act 1977, the Landlord and Tenant Act 1954 and the Housing Acts of 1985 and 1988. You must be familiar with these statutes and how they relate to each other. It is important to check carefully which statute applies to the tenancy in question. Reference should be made to specialist landlord and tenant texts for a detailed examination of these provisions. Most practitioners should carry a copy of *The Civil Court Practice* (Green Book), 1999, Butterworths or *The Civil Procedure Rules* (White Book), 1999, Sweet and Maxwell.

9.1.2 Basic procedure

Under the County Court Rules (CCR), possession proceedings were fixed date actions (CCR Ord 3, r 2). That procedure has now been abolished. The Practice Direction to CPR Pt 8 applies to proceedings for the recovery of possession of land. (PD 8, para B1(2)(a)). They must be commenced in the court for the district in which the property is situated. The particulars of claim in a possession action must be on one of the prescribed forms, which are listed in the Practice Direction supplementing Pt 4 (Table 3), and are the same as the old county court forms: Form N5 (summons for possession of property), Form N119 (possession proceedings including a claim for arrears of rent) and Form N120 (mortgage possession proceedings). The information which needs to be included in particulars of claim in possession proceedings is set out at CCR Ord 6, rr 3 and 5, in Sched 2 to the new rules. Since the prescribed forms have been retained, it would appear that there is no need for a statement of truth to be included, although one should perhaps include one out of an abundance of caution.

One problem with form N119 is that there is no specific provision for a claim for interest on arrears of rent. Such a claim should be added to box 9 on the form or a separate particulars of loss should be attached. Some judges refuse to award interest if it has not been included on the form. If you are representing the landlord, you should calculate the interest due to the date of the hearing in advance to present to the judge.

The county court has jurisdiction to hear and determine any action for the recovery of land. It has exclusive jurisdiction to hear certain possession actions. If you are to appear in the High Court, you should consider whether the High Court is the appropriate tribunal. Costs penalties may be imposed where the appropriate tribunal is in fact the county court. There is also a summary procedure which is appropriate in cases where the defendant is a trespasser or squatter (CCR Ord 24; RSC Ord 113).

Before appearing in court on an application for possession, you should ensure that your statements of case are in order and that any notice to quit which was served was in the proper form and stated the correct dates. If not, the hearing will have to be adjourned as the technicalities are normally strictly adhered to at trial.

Before appearing in possession proceedings, you should begin by establishing the following:

(1) the status of the occupier (for example, tenant, licensee or trespasser);

(2) the type of premises occupied (this will affect which statutory provisions, if any, apply);

(3) the nature of any tenancy or licence (different periods of notice will be required to determine the occupation);

(4) that the right to occupy has been brought to an end (where a notice to quit has been served, make sure that the form and period of notice are correct for the tenancy in question).

If acting on behalf of the Landlord, check that the following are available for the hearing (where appropriate):

- proof of title (the tenant will be estopped from denying the landlord's title, however, if the tenant does not turn up at court, you should be prepared to prove title);

- the original copy of the lease if the terms are to be relied upon;

- the tenancy agreement;

- a copy of the notice to quit;

- a proof of service of the notice to quit (this must be oral evidence of the person who effected service or with the leave of the court an affidavit or statements served pursuant to the Civil Evidence Act 1968 or 1995 – note that the 1995 Act repealed Pt 1 of the 1968 Act, but does not apply to proceedings commenced before 31 January 1997);

- if correspondence is to be relied upon, a notice to produce the original letter should be served on the other side;

- the landlord's record of the rent if this is in issue;

- satisfactory proof of the grounds upon which possession is sought or the breach of any covenant which will be relied on at the hearing.

This is important. In many cases, the landlord fails to appreciate the need for actual evidence of, for example deterioration of the property or nuisance caused to other tenants. These matters have to be pleaded and proved in the usual way. You should check that all witnesses have been asked to attend and photographs of the property are supplied where necessary.

9.1.3   Hearing

At the hearing, the court may proceed to hear the case and dispose of the claim or give case management directions, including allocating it to the appropriate track. The hearing of a possession order is a trial and therefore you should be familiar with the rules about evidence contained in Pt 32.

You should begin by introducing yourself and your opponent (if any) and state the nature of the claim. The judge may indicate that reference to the statements of case is unnecessary. You should then call your evidence straightaway. It is unusual for witness statements to be exchanged before the initial hearing and so, if the case is heard as a simple undefended matter, evidence will probably be oral (Pt 32.2(1)).

The landlord should give evidence to establish his title, the terms of the lease or tenancy agreement and the determination of the tenancy. He should produce any relevant documents while giving evidence. Make sure that you elicit evidence of, for example, the rent arrears or nuisance needed to prove the landlord's claim. If relevant, the landlord will have to prove the amount of rent payable and also the failure to pay. He will be allowed to refer to any record which he has kept in order to refresh his memory. If the record was not compiled by him, the provisions of the Civil Evidence Act 1995 must be complied with in order to adduce the evidence. The tenant will be given the opportunity to cross-examine if he wishes. You should know the amount of the arrears of rent and the mesne profits claimed. This will be stated as a daily sum in the particulars of claim and the court will require an up to date figure. In possession actions, do not forget to take a calculator into court.

The tenant is often unrepresented and, if appearing for the landlord, you should explain the procedure to the tenant. If settling a case, be sure that the tenant understands the nature of the landlord's claim and his rights in the particular case. Frequently, the tenant will not object to the claim for possession, but will want a court order so that he will not be 'intentionally homeless' in the eyes of the local authority when subsequently applying for council housing.

9.1.4   Alternative order

In certain cases, the court has the power to adjourn the proceedings, or on making a possession order, to stay or suspend the execution of the order, or postpone the date of possession (s 85 of the Housing Act 1985 or s 9 of the Housing Act 1988). The court will impose conditions to such on order, usually relating to the payment of the arrears of rent, unless it would cause hardship or be unreasonable. If a suspended order is granted, the tenant becomes a tolerated trespasser. A suspended order does not of itself determine the tenancy, but if the terms of the suspended order are breached by the tenant, then the tenancy is determined at that point, subject to the possibility that the tenancy may be revived if the tenant returns to compliance with the terms of the order.

9.1.5 Costs

Costs for possession actions are fixed. Refer to the table found at Pt II Appendix B to CCR Ord 38, Sched 2 to find the sum permitted.

9.2 Winding up petitions

The law regulating the winding up of companies by the court is set out in Chap VI of the Insolvency Act (IA 1986) and the Insolvency Rules (IR 1986). The main practitioner text on company law is *Palmer's Company Law,* Sweet & Maxwell, a looseleaf edition which is updated regularly. In addition, *Atkin's Court Forms,* Vol 10, 1995, Butterworths, sets out clearly in Table 5, pp 181-98 the steps to be taken in presenting a winding up petition.

9.2.1 The preliminaries

An advocate instructed to apply for a winding up order should have the following:

- a copy of the petition;
- an affidavit verifying the petition;
- a copy of the affidavit of service of the petition;
- a copy of the advertisement of the petition; and
- an indication of whether there are any creditors who either support or oppose the making of the order.

The advocate should ensure that the procedural requirements set out in the IR 1986 have been complied with. Principally, these are:

(1) that the petition is in order. Common defects are that the name of the company is incorrectly spelt or that the petition does not state which ground under s 122 of the IA 1986 is relied upon;

(2) that the affidavit verifying the petition is in order and complies with r 4.12 of the IR 1986. A copy of the petition should be exhibited to the affidavit. A common defect is to swear the affidavit of verification prior to the date of presentation of the petition. If this has happened, seek to obtain instructions that there was no material change between the date of swearing and the date of presentation. Alternatively, ensure that an affidavit re-verifying the petition is sworn;

(3) that the company has been properly served with the petition in accordance with r 4.8. This should be disclosed by the affidavit of service, and must comply with r 4.9 by exhibiting a copy of the petition and specifying with method of service prescribed by r 4.8 was used. If the affidavit is defective, ask the court for an adjournment to re-swear the affidavit (if the petition was properly served but the affidavit does not correctly state the facts or failed to specify the manner of service) or to effect re-service (if the petition has not been properly served);

(4) that the petition has been advertised in *The Gazette* in accordance with the provisions of r 4.11. Check in particular that:

   (a) the name of the company and address of its registered office are correct;

   (b) the date and venue and the name and address of the petitioner's solicitor are accurately stated;

   (c) it contains a notice informing any person intending to appear at the hearing that they should give notice of their intention in accordance with r 4.16. The petitioner's solicitor has a duty to prepare a list of the persons who have given such notice. The list must be handed in before the hearing. If it is not, the registrar will usually say 'There is no list' when the petition is called and refuse to proceed; and

   (d) that the petition was advertised at the correct time, that is, not less than seven business days before the hearing date and not less than seven business days after service of the petition on the company.

9.2.2 The hearing

In London, winding up petitions are listed for hearing before the Registrar of the Companies Court sitting in open court on Wednesday mornings at 10.30 am. Petitions are listed in 30 minute batches. The list of petitions is usually lengthy and may contain as many as 200 petitions in any one day. The Registrar is addressed as 'Sir'. Counsel and solicitors (properly robed) can appear at the hearing. The best way to learn how to apply for a compulsory winding up order is to attend at court and observe how it is done in practice.

If the petition is unopposed, the task is straightforward. After the name of the company to be wound up is called, you should stand and state to the court:

- the nature of the creditor or petitioner (for example, whether he is a trade creditor or a judgement creditor);
- the amount of the debt;
- whether the company is represented;
- whether there are any supporting creditors; and
- then ask for the usual compulsory order.

There is a standard form of words which is adopted:

> This is a trade creditor's petition based on a statutory demand in the sum of £1,789 odd. The company is not represented and the list is clear (or negative). I ask for the usual compulsory order.

Alternatively:

> This is a judgment creditor's petition based on a judgment debt, interest and costs in the sum of £10,867 odd. My learned friend Mr Toombs appears on behalf of the company. There is one supporting creditor and I ask for the usual compulsory order.

By convention, you do not state the number of pence which are owed but simply say £_____ odd.

9.2.3 Potential difficulties

Certificate of compliance

Under r 4.14, the petitioner or solicitor must lodge with the court, at least five days before the hearing of the petition, a certificate of due compliance showing the dates of the presentation, service, advertisement and hearing. The certificate must be lodged not later than 4.30 pm on the Friday before the hearing. If the registrar informs you that 'this is a certificate of compliance case', it means that a certificate has not been lodged. If this is the case, ask for leave to lodge the certificate out of time, and invite him to deal with the matter 'second time around'. The advocate can request that the defect be waived. If the court refuses, it will most likely adjourn the application for seven or 14 days to allow the certificate to be lodged properly.

Defective advertisement, petition or affidavit

If your application is defective in some way and you or the court staff have noticed it, do not ask for the usual compulsory order, but state the nature of the problem to the Registrar. Depending on the seriousness of the defect, he may be willing to waive it. Minor spelling mistakes in the petition or advertisement, defects in service (if the company has attended or if the petition has come to its attention) and minor breaches of the time limits in the rules are frequently waived. If the defect is not waived, you should ask for the petition to be stood over for a period of seven, 14, 21 or 28 days to enable the defect to be remedied. The length of time required will depend on the nature of the defect. If the petition has not been properly served, the whole process will have to begin again; if the advertisement is defective, a simple 14 day adjournment for re-advertisement will be sufficient.

If a petition has been adjourned before, you should give a brief history of the dates and the reasons for the adjournments at the outset of your address, for example:

> This trade creditor's petition was first before you, Sir, on 1 February when it was stood over to 15 February for re-advertisement. Unfortunately, advertisement had not been effected by that date and, accordingly, it was stood over again to today's date. Advertisement has now been effected. The company does not appear. The list is negative and I ask for the usual compulsory order.

Opposed petitions

If the company appears and simply seeks time for payment, the registrar usually grants a short adjournment of seven days to see if the matter can be resolved. If there are strong grounds of opposition to the petition, either from the company or an opposing creditor, the registrar will adjourn the matter for hearing before the judge of the Companies Court. Directions may be given for the filing of evidence and when the case is to be re-listed.

Substitution

If the petitioning creditor does not wish to pursue the petition, an application may be made by a supporting creditor to be substituted as petitioner and for the petition to continue.

10 Appeals

10.1 Rights of appeal

The following table indicates the main rights of appeal, but there are many other minor variations so it is important to check the CPR in particular cases.

Appeal from	*Appeal to*
County Court District Judge's Interim Order	County Court Judge
County Court District Judge's Final Order	County Court Judge
County Court Judge's Interim Order	Court of Appeal
County Court Judge's Final Order	Court of Appeal
High Court Master's Interim Order	Judge sitting in Private
High Court Master's Final Order	Court of Appeal
High Court District Judge's Interim Order	Judge sitting in Private
High Court District Judge's Final Order	Court of Appeal
High Court Judge's Interim Order	Court of Appeal
High Court Judge's Final Order	Court of Appeal
Employment Tribunal Decision	Employment Appeal Tribunal

10.2 Appeal to the Court of Appeal

The general procedure on appeal to the Court of Appeal, as set out in the Civil Procedure Rules and the Practice Direction for the Court of Appeal (Civil Division), is outlined below.

10.2.1 Permission to appeal

Permission to appeal to the Court of Appeal is required (of the court below or the Court of Appeal) for every appeal except an appeal against:

(a) the making of a committal order;

(b) a refusal to grant habeas corpus; or

(c) an order made under s 25 of the Children Act 1989 (secure accommodation orders) (RSC Ord 59 r 1B(1)(a)–(c)).

Where the parties are present for delivery of the judgment, it is routine for the judge below to ask whether either party wants to appeal and the matter will be dealt with there and then. Many applications to the Court of Appeal for permission to appeal are considered in first instance by a single Lord Justice on paper, but, in some cases, the application proceeds straight to an oral hearing.

The general rule is that permission to appeal will be granted unless an appeal would have no real prospect of success. Permission may also be given in exceptional circumstances even though the case has no real prospect of success, if there is an issue which, in the public interest, should be examined by the Court of Appeal. If the issues are not generally important and the costs of an appeal would far exceed what is at stake, that will be a factor which weighs against the grant of permission to appeal.

The appeal should be on a point of law which will materially affect the outcome of the case. An appeal on the grounds that there is no evidence to support a finding is an appeal on a point of law, but it is insufficient to show that there was little evidence. The Court of Appeal will rarely interfere with a decision based on the judge's evaluation of oral evidence as to the primary facts. Permission is more likely to be appropriate where what is being challenged is the inference which the judge has drawn from the primary facts. Further, the Court of Appeal will not interfere with the exercise of discretion by a judge unless satisfied the judge was wrong.

Where the application is for permission to appeal from an interim order, additional considerations arise:

(a) the point may not be of sufficient significance to justify the costs of an appeal;

(b) the procedural consequences of an appeal (for example, loss of the trial date) may outweigh the significance of the interim issue;

(c) it may be more convenient to determine the point at or after the trial.

In the former case, permission to appeal should be refused. In the latter two cases, it will be necessary to consider whether to refuse permission or adjourn the application until after the trial so as to preserve the appellant's right to appeal.

Where there has already been one unsuccessful appeal to a court (not a tribunal) against the decision being challenged (for example, from a District Judge to a Circuit Judge or from a Master to a High Court Judge), and the application is for permission for a further appeal to the Court of Appeal, a more restrictive approach to the test for permission to appeal is adopted. Permission should be granted only if the case raises a point of principle or practice or the case is one which for some other compelling reason should be considered by the Court of Appeal.

10.2.2 Notice of appeal

An appeal to the Court of Appeal is by way of rehearing and must be brought by notice of appeal, given either in respect of the whole or in respect of any specified part of the judgment or order of the court below. It must specify the grounds of the appeal and the precise form of the order sought. Permission is required of the Court of Appeal, a single judge or the registrar in order to rely on any grounds of appeal or to apply for any relief not so specified. The notice of appeal must also specify the list of appeals to which the appellant proposes that the appeal should be assigned (RSC Ord 59, r 3).

10.2.3 Time for appealing

Notice of appeal must generally be served not later than four weeks after the date on which the judgment or order of the court below was sealed or otherwise perfected (RSC Ord 59, r 4(1)).

Where permission to appeal is granted upon an application made within the four week period after the date on which the judgment or order of the court below was sealed or otherwise perfected, the notice of appeal may instead be served within seven days after the date when permission is granted (RSC Ord 58, r 4(3)).

Permission to appeal out of time can only be granted by application to the Court of Appeal in writing, setting out the reasons why permission should be granted and the reasons why the application was made out of time, unless the court otherwise directs (RSC Ord 59, rr 2C and 14(2)).

10.2.4   Setting down appeal

Within seven days after the date on which service of the notice of appeal was effected or, if later, the date on which the judgment or order of the court below was sealed or otherwise perfected, the appellant must set down his appeal by filing with the court the following:

- a copy of the relevant judgment or order; and
- two copies of the notice of appeal, one of which indorsed with the amount of the fee paid, and the other indorsed with a certificate of the date of service of the notice.

Within four days of receipt of notification from the office of the registrar that the appeal has been entered in the records of the court, the appellant must give notice to that effect to all parties on whom the notice of appeal was served, specifying the Court of Appeal reference allocated to that appeal (RSC Ord 59, r 5).

10.2.5   Respondent's notice

A respondent who, having been served with a notice of appeal, desires (a) to contend on the appeal that the decision of the court below should be varied, either in any event or in the event of the appeal being allowed in whole or in part; or (b) to contend that the decision of the court below should be affirmed on grounds other than those relied upon by that court; must give notice to that effect, specifying the grounds of his contention. In the case of the former, he must specify the precise form of order which he proposes to ask the court to make, and obtain permission to cross-appeal (unless the case falls within one of the three exceptions for which permission is not required) (RSC Ord 59, r 6(1)).

Permission is required in order to apply for any remedy not specified in the notice or to rely upon any ground not so specified or relied upon by the court below (RSC Ord 59, r 6(2)).

The respondent's notice must be served within 21 days after the notice of appeal on the respondent (RSC Ord 59, r 6(3)).

A party by whom a respondent's notice is given must, within four days after the date on which service of the respondent's notice was effected or, if later, the date on which he was notified that the appeal had been entered in the records of the court, file with the court two copies of the respondent's notice, one of which indorsed with the amount of the fee paid, and the other indorsed with a certificate of the date of service of the respondent's notice (RSC Ord 59, r 6(4)).

A contention that the decision of the court below was wrong in whole or in part is an appeal in its own right requiring permission.

10.2.6 Amendment of notice of appeal and respondent's notice

A notice of appeal or a respondent's notice may be amended by serving a supplementary notice before the appeal first appears in the Documents List, otherwise permission must be sought of the Court of Appeal, a single judge or the registrar Two copies of the supplementary notice must be filed at the court within two days after service (RSC Ord 59, r 7).

10.2.7 Filing of documents

Within 14 days of first appearing in the Document List, the appellant is required to file documents with the court in accordance with para 7.3 of the *Practice Direction for the Court of Appeal (Civil Division)* (RSC Ord 59, r 9).

10.3 Skeleton arguments

10.3.1 Skeleton arguments for permission to appeal

Applications for permission to appeal must be accompanied by skeleton arguments and where dates are significant, a chronology must be filed at the same time. If practicable, the chronology should be agreed with the respondent.

If the application for permission is listed for an oral hearing with both sides in attendance, the respondent must file and serve its skeleton argument within 14 days of receipt of the applicant's bundle.

10.3.2   Skeleton arguments for the main appeal

If permission is granted to appeal by the single Lord Justice, on consideration of the papers, he may give directions as to the maximum time to be allowed to each party for oral argument on the appeal and as to the filing and service of skeleton arguments for the substantive appeal.

Four copies of an appellant's skeleton must be included with the appeal bundles. Four copies of a respondent's skeleton must be lodged within 21 days of being served with the appeal bundle, or, if earlier, not later than 14 days before the appeal hearing.

No supplementary skeleton arguments may be filed without the permission of the Court. Permission will only be granted if there are good reasons for doing so.

10.3.3   Content of the skeleton argument

The skeleton arguments should contain a numbered list of the points which the advocate proposes to argue, stated in no more than one or two sentences. Each listed point should be followed by full references to the material to which the advocate will refer in support of it. It should also contain anything which the advocate would expect to be taken down by the court during the hearing, such as propositions of law, chronologies of events, lists of characters and, where necessary, glossaries of terms.

A skeleton argument should be as succinct as possible. In the case of a normal length appeal against a final order, skeleton arguments should not normally exceed 10 pages in the case of an appeal on law and 15 pages in the case of an appeal on fact.

In the case of points of law, the skeleton argument should state the point and cite the principle authority or authorities in support, with references to particular page(s) where the principle concerned is enunciated. In the case of questions of fact, it should state briefly the basis on which it is contended that the Court of Appeal can interfere with the finding of fact concerned, with cross-references to the passages in the transcript or notes of evidence which bear on the point.

11 Costs

11.1 Introduction

One of the fundamental aims behind the new Rules was to make litigation more affordable to a wider section of society than was the case under the old rules. Another aim was to make the costs of litigation more predictable so that litigants could be informed of the costs that they were likely to incur in proceeding with a claim at a relatively early stage in the process. The means of achieving these objectives are as follows:

- the threshold for small claims has been increased to £5,000, so that more cases can be dealt with by arbitration, with fixed costs (CPR r 27.14);

- cases allocated to the fast track are subject to limited fixed trial costs (CPR Pt 46);

- the courts take a more active role in case management to focus the parties' attention on the real issues and to ensure that cases proceed to trial as quickly as possible;

- the parties' solicitors have to provide an estimate of total costs in the allocation questionnaire.

We first consider legal aid, and then more general principles of costs. For further details, consult *The Civil Procedure Rules* and *Blackstone's Guide to the Civil Procedure Rules*.

11.2 Legal aid

11.2.1 General scheme

A solicitor is under a professional duty, enforceable both by disciplinary sanction and by action for damages, to consider whether a client is eligible for legal aid and to give him appropriate advice about it. This duty is owed even if the solicitor habitually does not undertake legal aid work, and the solicitor must keep under review the possibility that a client who was not initially eligible might become so following a change in circumstances. There are essentially three different types of legal aid available in civil cases:

• the Green Form Scheme;

• the Advice By Way of Representation (ABWOR) scheme;

• the full Civil Legal Aid Scheme.

All three types of legal aid are means tested.

11.2.2 Legal Advice and Assistance (the Green Form Scheme)

This scheme covers advice and help with any legal problems, including giving general advice, writing letters, negotiating, obtaining counsel's opinion and preparing a written case to go before a tribunal. It covers all assistance short of actual representation and extends to most legal problems concerning English law, such as divorce or maintenance. It enables those who are eligible for such assistance to obtain help from a solicitor for up to two hours' worth of work (or three in matrimonial cases involving the preparation of a petition). If solicitors need to do more work, they cannot claim for it without the permission of the area office. If it appears that a client may need to proceed to court in civil proceedings, generally, it will be necessary to apply for civil legal aid or ABWOR. In a criminal case, it will generally be necessary to apply for criminal legal aid. Legal Advice and Assistance is available in England and Wales. It applies only to matters of English law. It does not cover the law of Scotland, Northern Ireland nor of any other country.

Legal Advice and Assistance is the simplest and most limited of the form of legal aid available. It covers the solicitor's initial advice; assistance in obtaining evidence; negotiating settlements; writing letters, obtaining counsel's opinion and the like, but it does not extend to taking any steps in proceedings in court.

The means test adopted is simple and is carried out by the solicitor himself on the basis of information supplied by the client. The solicitor is then able to incur expenditure, whether in the form of costs or disbursements, up to the equivalent of the charge allowed for two hours' preparation work, or three hours in cases of divorce and judicial separation, involving the preparation of a petition. This is subject to a maximum of £136.50 outside London, £144.75 in London for franchisees and £132.00 outside London and £139.50 in London for non-franchisees (as of 6 April 1998). The solicitor can apply to the area office of the Legal Aid Board for authority to extend this, but this cannot be given retrospectively. It is therefore important that the solicitor monitors the amount of expenditure incurred on a Green Form and applies for extensions before the previous limit has been reached. Depending on their financial position, some clients have to contribute to the fees incurred on legal aid.

11.2.3 The ABWOR scheme

This scheme was grafted on to the Legal Advice and Assistance scheme in order to enable solicitors to provide their clients with representation in a limited number of areas, such as the Mental Health Review Tribunal and certain proceedings in the magistrates or county courts, but not such common tribunals as the Employment Tribunal or any of the social security tribunals. The means test is the same as for Legal Advice and Assistance. Application for ABWOR is made by the solicitor to the Legal Aid Board and the resulting ABWOR certificate covers only the work described in the certificate: there is no financial limit on the work which the solicitor is authorised to do.

11.2 4 Civil legal aid

This is the most comprehensive of the types of legal aid available in civil cases and enables a solicitor to provide a complete service of representation to a client in all courts from the county court to the House of Lords. Proceedings of a civil nature in the magistrates' or Crown Court, such as care proceedings, are usually covered by the criminal legal aid scheme. The only tribunal presently within the scope of the Civil Legal Aid Scheme is the Employment Appeal Tribunal. Almost all types of civil case are potentially covered by the scheme, the most notable exclusion being proceedings for defamation and undefended divorce petitions.

Application is made by the client, usually via the solicitor, to the Legal Aid Board. The Board determines whether the client has a reasonable case and one which justifies the expenditure of legal aid money. The test determines whether the client has a reasonable case and one which justifies the expenditure of legal aid money. The test is whether 'a man of modest means' would, in the absence of legal aid, decide to proceed with the litigation. If the claim is for a sum of money not exceeding £500, legal aid will almost certainly be refused on the ground that, even if the client were successful, he would be unlikely to recover his costs from the other side and the prosecution or defence of the claim cannot therefore be justified on economic grounds. It may also be refused where the amount in issue is higher if the claim is unlikely to be economic. In addition, legal aid will be refused if, even if the client were successful, he is unlikely to be able to recover his costs from the other party. A 'means test' is carried out by the Department of Social Security. A current eligibility table can be found in *The Legal Aid Handbook 1998–99* (Sweet & Maxwell).

If the client's means are within the relevant limits and if the Board is prepared to grant legal aid on the merits, a Certificate is issued. This process usually takes some months and (albeit rarely) has been known to take over a year. It is vital to appreciate that a Legal Aid Certificate is only effective from the date when it is issued, and that any work done *before* the certificate is issued will have to be covered either by a Legal Advice and Assistance or, where the client has agreed to pay privately until the grant of legal aid, by a private bill to the client. In urgent cases, an Emergency Certificate can be obtained from the Board, and in really urgent cases this can be done over the telephone. The Emergency Certificate is effective immediately but the work which it authorises is often limited to a particular step such as obtaining an injunction.

All Legal Aid Certificates, whether emergency or substantive, can carry limitations or conditions and, if they are not complied with, the costs of any unauthorised work will be disallowed. If a certificate is limited in extent to, for example, covering an action down to close of statements of case, an amendment can be obtained from the Board to authorise further work to be done. It is important to note that a claimant granted leave to prosecute a matter still has to apply separately for leave to defend a Part 20 claim since this is not covered in the original certificate.

On the refusal of an application, appeal can be made to the Area Legal Aid Committee. If any work is disallowed on a detailed assessment as being outside the scope of legal aid cover, the client cannot generally be asked to pay for it. Consequently, solicitors and counsel must satisfy themselves that the work which they are doing is authorised by the Legal Aid Certificate and, to enable counsel to do this, solicitors are obliged to place copies of all Legal Aid Certificates, amendments etc, in their instructions to counsel.

11.2.5 The 'statutory charge'

If money or property is recovered or preserved as a result of work carried out under any of the forms of legal aid, the Legal Aid Board has a first charge on such money or such property to the extent of the legal costs payable by the Board. The solicitor is under a duty to advise the client from the outset about the application of the charge in his case. If counsel does not appreciate the application of the charge, he may well advise a settlement which on its face is favourable to the client but is a disaster when the implications of the statutory charge are taken into account.

In legal aid cases, there can be two strands of costs orders running through the case, one dealing exclusively with the right of the solicitor to make a charge against the Legal Aid Fund, and the other regulating the awards of costs payable by one party to the other: for example, 'No order for costs. Legal Aid Taxation of the Claimant's Costs'. The first part of the order is dealing with the costs payable by one side to the other, and the second part is dealing with the legal aid costs.

11.2.6 Court's discretion and circumstances to be taken into account when exercising its discretion as to costs

CPR r 44.3(1) provides that the court has discretion as to:
* whether costs are payable by one party to another;
* the amount of costs to be paid; and
* when costs are to be paid.

The general rule is that the unsuccessful party will be ordered to pay the costs of the successful party, (apart from in the exceptional cases specified in CPR r 44.3(3)), but the court may make a different order.

In deciding what order to make about costs, the court will have regard to all the circumstances, including:
* the conduct of all the parties;
* whether a party has succeeded on part of his case, even if he has not been wholly successful; and
* any payment into court or admissible offer to settle made by a party which is drawn to the court's attention (whether or not made in accordance with Pt 36).

When considering the conduct of the parties, the court will take into account:

- conduct before, as well as during, the proceedings and the extent to which the parties followed any relevant pre-action protocol;
- whether it was reasonable for a party to raise, pursue or contest a particular allegation or issue; and
- whether a claimant who has succeeded in his claim, in whole or in part, exaggerated his claim.

There are various different types of order that the court can make, which are listed at CPR r 44.3 (6), for example, an order that a party must pay a proportion of another party's costs, or costs from or until a specified date or costs relating to a distinct part of the proceedings.

11.2.7   Basis of assessment of costs

Under CPR 44.7, when the court makes a costs order, it may either:

- make a summary assessment of the costs; or
- order a detailed assessment by a costs officer (that is, a costs judge, a district judge or an authorised court officer – see CPR 43.2 for definitions).

11.3 Summary assessment

'Assessment' is the new term for taxation of costs. If a summary assessment of costs is undertaken, the court will determine the amount of costs to be paid at the end of the hearing. This will not involve detailed and precise calculations, but rather an approximation of the sums involved. The general rule is that the court will make a summary assessment of the costs at the conclusion of a case which has been dealt with on the fast track (in which case the order will deal with the costs of the whole claim), and at the conclusion of any other hearing which has lasted for less than a day (in which case the order will deal with the costs of the application or matter to which the hearing related) (PD 44, para 4.3).

For interim applications and fast track trials, parties are required to file a statement of their costs, in the form of a schedule, with the court, and to serve a copy on any party against whom an order for payment of these costs is intended to be sought, not less than 24 hours before the hearing. PD 44, para 4.5 sets out the form and contents of a statement of costs and a precedent is provided in the Schedule of costs forms (Form 1). The court may not make a summary assessment of the costs of a receiving party who is legally aided or who is a child or patient within

Pt 21 (unless the solicitor acting for the child or patient has waived the right to further costs). Further, where an order is made for costs in the case (formerly 'costs in the cause'), it will usually not be appropriate for summary assessment to take place (PD 44, para 4.4(3)). Generally, it seems that the courts are taking a conservative approach when determining the sum to be awarded. The court may ask for evidence, if it is available, to justify the costs claimed and, on some occasions, may request assistance from the winning party's solicitor.

11.3.1 Detailed assessment

Detailed assessment is the new term for 'taxation' of costs under the old rules. It will usually not take place until the conclusion of the proceedings (see PD 47, para 1.1 for further details). However, the court has the power to order detailed assessment at an earlier stage, for example if there is no realistic prospect of the claim proceeding (PD 47, para 1.1(4)). If there is an appeal pending, the assessment will not be stayed, unless the court makes an order to that effect (PD 47, para 1.2).

Generally, the court has a discretion as to which form of assessment should be ordered, in the event that costs cannot be agreed. Where, however, the party is a child or a patient, the court must order a detailed assessment of costs (CPR 48.5(2)(a)), unless one of the exceptions listed at PD 48, para 1.4 applies.

The procedure for detailed assessment of costs is set out in Pt 47, supplemented by PD 47. It is not within the scope of this book to deal with this.

11.3.2 'Standard' and 'indemnity' costs

Cost can be assessed on the 'standard' or the 'indemnity' basis. When the court is assessing costs, individual items of costs will be considered to determine whether they were reasonably incurred and whether the full or a reduced amount should be allowed. Costs orders should specify the intended basis of quantification. Where there is no indication, the costs will be assessed on the standard basis (CPR 44.4(4)(a)). In general, costs will be assessed on the standard basis. Parties acting in the capacity of trustee, mortgagee or personal representative are generally entitled to costs on an indemnity basis, unless the party has acted for a benefit other than for that of the fund (CPR 48.4)

11.3.3   Standard basis

Pursuant to CPR 44.4(2), where the amount of costs is to be assessed on the standard basis, the court will:

- only allow costs which are proportionate to the matters in issue; and
- resolve any doubt which it may have as to whether costs were reasonably incurred or reasonable and proportionate in amount in favour of the paying party.

The court will have regard to all the circumstances in determining whether the costs were proportionately and reasonably incurred and proportionate and reasonable in amount (CPR 44.5(a)).

PD 44, para 3.1 to 3.2 sets out the factors to be taken into account in deciding the amount of costs to be awarded. The following points should be noted:

- the relationship between the total costs incurred and the financial total of the claim may not be a reliable guide;
- in any proceedings there will be costs which will inevitably be incurred and which are necessary for the successful conduct of the case;
- solicitors are not required to carry out litigation at uneconomic rates;
- the time taken by the court in dealing with a particular issue at trial may not be an accurate guide to the amount of time properly spent preparing that issue for trial.

11.3.4   Indemnity basis

On an assessment on the indemnity basis, there is no reference to proportionality. As under the former system, the onus is on the paying party to show that costs were unreasonably incurred or unreasonable in amount.

11.3.5   Interim orders for costs

The provisions relating to interim costs orders are to be found in PD 44. If an order makes no reference to costs, none are payable in respect of the proceedings to which the order relates (CPR 44.13(1). The court may make an order about costs at any stage in a case, and when dealing with interim applications, it may make interim costs orders. The most frequently used costs orders are defined at PD 44, para 2 and are as follows.

Costs/costs in any event

This order means that the party in whose favour the order is made is entitled to the costs in respect of the part of the proceedings to which the order relates, whatever other costs orders are made in the proceedings.

Costs in the case/costs in the application

The consequence of this order is that the party in whose favour the court makes an order for costs at the end of proceedings is entitled to his costs of the part of the proceedings to which the order relates.

Costs reserved

If this order is made, the decision about costs will be deferred to a later occasion, but if no later order is made, the order will be costs in the case.

Claimant's/defendant's costs in the case/application

With this order, if the party in whose favour the costs order is made is awarded costs at the end of the proceedings, that party is entitled to his costs of the part of the proceedings to which the order relates. If any other party is awarded costs at the end of the proceedings, the party in whose favour the final costs order is made is not liable to pay the costs of any other party in respect of the part of the proceedings to which the order relates.

Costs thrown away

The effect of this order is that where, for example, a judgment or order is set aside, the party in whose favour the costs order is made is entitled to the costs which have been incurred as a consequence. This includes costs of:

(a) preparing for and attending any hearing at which the judgment or order which has been set aside was made;

(b) preparing for and attending any hearing to set aside the judgment or order in question;

(c) preparing for and attending any hearing at which the court order the proceedings or the part in question to be adjourned; and

(d) any steps taken to enforce a judgment or order which has subsequently been set aside.

Costs of and caused by

The example given in the definition of this order is where the court makes this order on an application to amend a statement of case, the party in whose favour the costs order is made is entitled to the costs of preparing for and attending the application and the costs of any consequential amendment to his own statement of case.

Costs here and below

Where this order is made, the party in whose favour the costs order is made is entitled not only to his own costs in respect of the proceedings in which the court makes the order but also to his costs of the proceedings in any lower court. In the case of an appeal from a Divisional Court, the party is not entitled to any costs incurred in any court below the Divisional Court.

No order as to costs/each party to pay his own costs

If this order is made, each party is to bear his own costs of the part of the proceedings to which the order relates whatever costs order the court makes at the end of the proceedings.

11.3.6 Assessment of interim costs

The general rule is that costs of interim hearings likely to last less than a day will be dealt with by way of summary assessment at the conclusion of the hearing, unless there is good reason not to do so, for example, there is insufficient time to carry out a summary assessment.

11.3.7 Fixed costs

Fixed costs are dealt with in Pt 45. Where the fixed costs provisions apply, the claimant is entitled to recover, in addition to the substantive remedy, the court fee paid on issue plus the fixed costs which are set out in the tables in CPR Pt 45 and RSC Ord 62, Appendix 3, or CCR Ord 38, Appendix B. CPR 45.1(2) sets out the instances where fixed costs apply, which include where summary judgment is given under Pt 24 and where judgment in default is obtained under r 12.4(1). In a small claims track case, the fixed costs payable to the claimant are the fixed costs calculated in accordance with Table 1 of r 45. 2 and the appropriate court fee or fees paid by the claimant (PD 45, para 1.2).

11.3.8 Fast track trial costs

Fast track costs are dealt with by Pt 46 and apply to the cost of an advocate for preparing for and appearing at the trial of claim in the fast track. These rules only apply where, at the date of trial, the claim has been allocated to the fast track. It does not apply in any other case, regardless of the financial value of the claim (PD 46, para 1.1 and 1.2). Where a case that has been allocated to the fast track settles before the commencement of the trial, when deciding the sum to which the advocate is entitled for his preparation, the court will take into account when the case settled and when the court was notified that the case had settled. The sum awarded must not be in excess of the fixed trial costs which would have been payable had the trial taken place.

The fast track trial costs which the court may award are set out at r 46.2 and are as follows:

VALUE OF THE CLAIM	AMOUNT OF FAST TRACK TRIAL COST WHICH THE COURT MAY AWARD
Up to £3,000	£350
More than £3,000 but no more than £10,000	£500
More than £10,000	£750

For a successful claimant, the value of the claim is the amount of the judgment excluding interest, costs and any reduction for contributory negligence. For a successful defendant, it is the amount the claimant specified on the claim form (r 46.2(3)).

The court may not award more or less than the amount shown in the table except where:

- it decides not to award any fast track trial costs; or
- it decides to award fast track trial costs to a party's legal representative who attended the trial in addition to the advocate, where that attendance was necessary to assist the advocate (for which a sum of £250 may be awarded); or
- the court decides it is necessary to direct a separate trial of an issue, in which case the court may award an additional amount in respect

of the separate trial (but it must not exceed two-thirds of the amount payable for that claim): see CPR 46.2(2) and 46.3(2)–(4).

Rule 46.3(6) explains how the total value is calculated according to the various results that can arise out of a counterclaim and r 46.4(4)–(6) deals with cases where there are multi-claimants or defendants.

11.4 Part 36 payment or offer

This is a complex departure from the usual rule that the unsuccessful party will be ordered to pay the costs of the successful party. If the defendant makes a Part 36 payment (in respect of a money claim) and/or or a Part 36 offer (in respect of a non-money claim), which is accepted by the claimant, the action is stayed and the claimant is entitled to the costs of the action up to the date of the notice of acceptance of the Part 36 payment or offer. However, the Part 36 payment or offer puts the claimant under great pressure because if he does not accept the payment or offer, but at trial is awarded a sum less than or equal to the amount of the Part 36 payment or offer, not only will he not gain costs against the defendant for the period after the latest date on which the Part 36 payment or offer could have been accepted, but he will actually have to pay the defendant his costs of that period, unless the court considers it unjust to make such an order (CPR 36.20(2)).

The claimant will be awarded his costs down to the date of the serving of acceptance, but these may not even equal the costs which the defendant is awarded against him. It is only if the trial judge awards him more than the amount of the payment into court that the claimant will recover the costs of the whole action. In this connection, it is important to note that trial judge is not told about the payment until all questions of liability and the amount of money to be awarded have been decided. If a Part 36 offer or payment which relates only to part of the claim is accepted, unless the parties have agreed costs, the liability for costs shall be decided by the court.

Where a claimant's Part 36 offer is accepted without needing the permission of the court, the claimant will be entitled to his costs of the proceedings up to the date on which the defendant serves notice of acceptance: CPR 36.14. In the event, that the claimant does better than he proposed in his Part 36 offer, the court may make an order that he is entitled to his costs on an indemnity basis from the latest date when the defendant could have accepted the offer and interest on those costs at a rate not exceeding 10% above base rate: CPR 36.21(3).

11.5 Security for costs

The provision for security for costs can be found in CPR Sched 1 which re-enacts RSC Ord 23. This order applies to proceedings in the High Court and the county court. Under r 1, the grounds for requiring security for costs are:

- the claimant is ordinarily resident out of the jurisdiction; or
- the claimant is a nominal claimant who is suing for the benefit of some other person and there is reason to believe that he will be unable to pay the costs of the defendant if ordered to do so; or
- the claimant's address is not stated or is incorrectly stated in the claim form or other originating process (unless it was an innocent mistake and there was no intention to deceive); or
- the claimant has changed his address during the course of the proceedings to evade the consequences of litigation.

Having regard to all the circumstances of the case, if the court thinks it just to do so, it may order the claimant to provide security for the defendant's costs of the proceedings in a sum which is considered to be fair. A claimant may also make an application for security for costs against a defendant with a counterclaim.

11.6 Awards of costs in tribunals

A successful party in an employment tribunal rarely obtains an order for costs from the other side, nor is legal aid available for tribunal hearings. For that reason, parties are often forced to take a 'commercial view' and to make or accept an offer of settlement to save the cost of the matter proceeding to a hearing, or in the event that it does proceed to a hearing, will try to keep costs to a minimum.

It is only in the following exceptional cases that a successful party will be awarded its costs in an employment tribunal:

- if the unsuccessful party has, in the opinion of the tribunal, acted frivolously, vexatiously, abusively, disruptively or otherwise unreasonably in bringing or conducting proceedings (Employment Tribunal Rules 1993, r 12(1)). It is the conduct of the party, rather than that of his legal representative which must be considered when an order for costs is being contemplated;
- if a hearing has to be postponed or adjourned through the fault of the other party.

In complaints of unfair dismissal where:

- the applicant has expressed a wish to be reinstated or re-engaged and has communicated that wish to the respondent at least seven days before the date of the hearing; or

- the proceedings arise out of the respondent's failure to permit the applicant to return to work after an absence due to pregnancy or confinement,

then an order for costs must be made if the proceedings have to be adjourned or postponed due to the respondent's failure, without special reason, to adduce evidence as to the availability of the job from which the employee was dismissed or which she held before her absence, or of comparable or suitable employment (r 12(5)).

In making an order for costs, the tribunal must have regard to the means of the party against whom the order is made. The tribunal should not have regard to the means of any body, such as a trade union which may have supported the applicant in the proceedings. If as a result of a pre-hearing review, a deposit was ordered, this will be set off against any order for costs made subsequently.

12 Useful Addresses

Central Office of Employment Tribunals
19–29 Woburn Place
London WC1H 0LU
020 7273 8666

Criminal Injuries Compensation Authority
Morley House
26–30 Holborn Viaduct
London WC1A 2JQ
020 7842 6800

Employment Appeal Tribunal
Audit House
58 Victoria Embankment
London EC4Y 0DS
020 7273 1041

Immigration Appeals Authority
Taylor House
88 Rosebery Avenue
London EC1R 4QU
020 7862 4200

Independent Tribunals Service (including Social Security,
   Medical and Disability Appeal Tribunals)
4th Floor
Whittington House
19–30 Alfred Place
London WC1E 7LW
020 7814 6500

Land Tribunal
48–49 Chancery Lane
London WC2A 1SR
020 7936 7200

Mental Health Review Tribunal
Block 1
Spur 3
Canon's Park Government Buildings
Honeypot Lane
Stanmore
Middlesex HA7 1AY
020 7972 2000

The Royal Courts of Justice
The Strand
London WC2A 2CC
020 7936 6000

Value Added Tax and Duties Tribunal
15–19 Bedford Avenue
London WC1B 3AS
020 7631 4242

13 Further Reading

Advocacy

Boulton, W (Sir), *Conduct and Etiquette at the Bar*, 1975, London: Butterworths.

Du Cann, R, *Art of the Advocate*, 1982, London: Penguin.

Evans, K, *Advocacy at the Bar*, 1993, London: Blackstone.

Napley, D, *The Technique of Persuasion*, 1983, London: Sweet & Maxwell.

The Courts

Blackstone's Court Guide, 1998, London: Blackstone.

Goodman, A, *Guide to the Royal Courts of Justice*, 1997, Legastat.

Practice and Procedure

Archbold, *Criminal Pleading: Evidence and Practice*, London: Sweet & Maxwell.

Atkins Court Forms (updated service), London: Butterworths.

Blake, S, *A Practical Approach to Legal Advice and Drafting*, 1989, London: Blackstone.

Bourne, C, Popat, P and Gilliatt, J, *Civil Advocacy: A Practical Guide*, 2nd edn, 2000, London: Cavendish Publishing.

Bowers, J, Brown, D and Mead, E, *Employment Tribunal Practice*, 1999, London: Sweet & Maxwell.

Bullen, E, Leake, S and Jacob, J (Sir), *Precedents: Principles and Practice* (updated service), London: Sweet & Maxwell.

Chitty, T and Jacob, I (eds), *Queen's Bench Forms* (updated work), London: Sweet & Maxwell.

Coswill, E and Clegg, J, *Evidence: Law and Practice*, 1987, London: Longman.

Foskett, D, *The Law and Practice of Compromise*, 1994, London: Sweet & Maxwell.

Gerlis, S, *Practice Notes: County Court Procedure*, 1996, London: Cavendish Publishing.

Gordon, R, *Judicial Review: Law and Practice*, 1985, London: Sweet & Maxwell.

Matthews, P and Malek, H, *Discovery*, 1992, London: Sweet & Maxwell.

Odgers, W, *Principles on Pleading and Practice in Civil Actions,* 1981, London: Sweet & Maxwell.

Salter, D and Evans, D (eds), *Longman Litigation Practice* (updated service), London: Longman.

Shaw, N, *Effective Advocacy*, 1996, London: Sweet & Maxwell.

Stones Justices' Manual (updated service), 3 Vols, 1989, London: Butterworths.

Style, C and Hollander, C, *Documentary Evidence*, 1987, London: Longman.

Specialist Publications

Bean, D, *Injunctions*, 1996, London: Longman.

Birks, H, *Practice Notes: Contentious Costs*, 1998, London: Cavendish Publishing.

Bowers, J, *Bowers on Employment Law*, 1996, London: Blackstone.

Colbey, R, *Practice Notes: Residential Tenancies*, 1996, London: Cavendish Publishing.

Davidson, R and Webber, G, *Residential Possession Proceedings*, 3rd edn, 1990, London: Longman.

Frieze, S, *Compulsory Winding Up Procedure*, 1987, London: Longman.

Goldrein and Wilkinson, *Commercial Litigation: Pre-emptive Remedies*, 1996, London: Sweet & Maxwell.

Josling, J, *Periods of Limitation*, 1986, London: Longman.

Law: Landlord and Tenant (updated service), London: Sweet & Maxwell.

Legal Aid Handbook 1989, 1989, London: HMSO.

O'Hare, J and Hill, R, *Civil Litigation*, 7th edn, 1996, London: FT Law &Tax.

Practical Commercial Precedents (updated service), 1989, London: Longman.

Rajak, H, *Company Liquidations*, 1988, CCH Editions.

Tolley's Company Law, 1988, London: Tolley.

Vaulkhard, S, *Legal Aid*, 1989, London: Longman.

Wilkinson's Road Traffic Offences, 1989, London: Longman.